The Incredible Tests 1981

The Incredible Tests 1981

IAN BOTHAM

Pelham Books   London

First published in Great Britain by
Pelham Books Ltd
44 Bedford Square
London WC1B 3DU
1981

ISBN 0 7207 1394 3

Typeset, printed and bound in Great Britain
by Fakenham Press Limited,
Fakenham, Norfolk

Contents

Acknowledgements

I would like to thank Peter Smith for invaluable assistance in writing this book, Bill Frindall for compiling a statistical summary of the series and Adrian Murrell (of Allsport) and Ken Kelly for the photographs.

Adrian Murrell: pages 16, 21, 22, 26, 57, 58, 60, 63, 68, 72 (above), 74, 77 (both), 82 (both), 84, 85, 92 (above), 96, 97, 102, 111, 116 (both), 119 (both), 127 (both), 128 (both), 131, 132, 144, 146, 147.

Ken Kelly: frontispiece, pages 40 (all), 66, 67, 72 (below), 92 (below), 94, 98 (both), 100, 101, 103, 104 (both), 112, 129, 137, 138, 139, 143.

1 Summer of discontent
-and satisfaction

Big boys are not supposed to cry. Standing two inches over six foot and tipping the scales at a weight that some people apparently find alarming, but that I find both comfortable and necessary, I am a big boy. I didn't cry during the remarkable summer of '81, but I have to confess there were times when I was driven very close to tears. Not only out of anger, frustration and disappointment, but also out of a feeling of joy and delight. It was that kind of a summer – particularly for me.

The tears in my family were shed by my wife Kath, which accounted for my anger, frustration and disappointment. And it was all because I was placed in an intolerable position when appointed match by match as England's captain at the start of the Ashes series against Australia.

It was a cruel public trial played out before a jury of many thousands. A trial that I accepted at the start for the first Test at Trent Bridge because leading my country into battle on the cricket field means so much to me. Yet I was forced to reject it in the end when I resigned after the second Test at Lord's. I did so because I could see the disastrous effect the public examination of my ability to lead was having on my family and on the team I was supposed to inspire and command.

The family life of a cricketer during the summer months in England is not much to write home about. Perhaps I can snatch a few hours in my own home up in South Humberside when Somerset have no match and I can actually say more than a quick 'hello' and 'goodbye' to the children I have missed growing up. Perhaps we have the odd evening in the team's hotel when my wife and the children have been able to get away and join me on my travels around the country. These should be rare moments to treasure, an attempt to get together as a family unit just like ninety-nine per cent of the married couples in the world. Unfortunately, the memory of the times Kath and I were together during the early part of summer 1981 is one of anxiety and distress over Kath's health. In a month she lost almost a stone in weight from the beating she took because the selectors did not have enough faith in me to see the job through against Australia. I had to part company with the captaincy for her sake as well as for my own peace of mind and for the good of the players around me.

Those were the black moments of 1981, the ones I want to wipe from my mind. The memory, for instance, of walking away from the wicket at Lord's after bagging a 'pair' to be met by a stony silence from the MCC members as I climbed up the pavilion steps and waited for the famous Long Room to swallow me from sight. It was a walk I doubt whether I shall ever forget however much I try.

What I *shall* never forget, or wish to forget, was my reception one Test match later when I walked back to the dressing-room at Headingley after scoring my first Test century of the summer. Or the crowd at Edgbaston when I took five wickets for one run to help England to their second victory. Or the congratulations heaped on my back as I walked through the members at Old Trafford on my return from the crease after my second century which helped to clinch the series.

Threading their way up the steps through the Lancashire members is an experience players have been known to fear. The comments and insults hurled at some players led one journalist to christen the area the 'pit of hate'. The sun was shining brightly on that third day of the fifth Test yet I could still feel the warmth and affection from the crowd. That was a moment when tears of joy and happiness were only just kept below the surface.

Yes, a remarkable summer for both me and England. People will forever insist that there is a link between my blackest moment at Lord's and my brightest at Old Trafford. At Lord's I was England's captain and had behind me a string of failures with the bat which started when I was first handed the role. At Old Trafford I was no longer captain, Mike Brearley had assumed control once more. I was back among the wickets and the runs came again for my country.

Not once during my twelve-match reign as England's cricketing leader had I collected five wickets in an innings, although I had achieved that feat on fourteen other occasions before taking charge. Not once during my time leading England did I collect a Test match century – my highest score being 57 in my first Test as captain against the West Indies at Trent Bridge in 1980. Not once did I manage to steer England to victory in the twelve Tests when I was in command, a record unmatched by any other Test captain in the history of the game.

Suddenly I was just one of the boys again, an ordinary member of the ranks having given away my commission. The wickets were there again, the runs flowing freely once more. Six wickets in an innings combined with a half century and a century at Headingley ... five wickets in an innings at Edgbaston ... a century at Old Trafford ... six wickets in an innings at The Oval. The catches were sticking too. There was enough evidence to support the argument that it was not just coincidence. Even Mike Brearley – somebody I admire both as a person and a captain and whose judgment I respect – came round to that point of view. This is one occasion when I will take issue with him.

If I thought for one moment that leading England in Test matches affected me as a player or as a person I would not want the job back, however much it must remain the ambition of every cricketer to captain his country. But let me make it clear here and now – I *do* want the job back.

Keith Fletcher was given the captaincy at the end of the Test series and I will do everything in my power to make sure he keeps it as long as possible. I shall serve him to the best of my ability in exactly the same way I served Mike. But when Keith loses the captaincy or decides he no longer wishes to continue in the role, I hope the selectors then in charge will turn to me first.

I do not consider for one moment that I was a failure as captain in the two series against the West Indies. We did not win either series, but nobody really expected us to in what has been described as the toughest twelve months any team could have faced against the acknowledged world champions in all facets of the game both at home and away. Immediately before tackling us Clive Lloyd's team had annihilated Greg Chappell's side in Australia – the same Australian side which had beaten England led by Mike 3–0.

I admit I was a novice as a captain. My captaincy experience had been limited to a couple of occasions at school and leading England against Queensland in Brisbane on the 1979–80 tour of Australia. Yet you can't help picking up some of the finer points of the game when serving under Mike as I had done, especially standing close to him in the slips so that I was always familiar with his thinking and how he interpreted the way games were progressing.

I believe I knew enough about the game to make a leader in tactics and technique. I also believe I knew enough about handling people to make a good commander, especially by the end of that first summer. However, to be successful, especially when the odds are stacked against you in tackling one of the finest sides the game has ever produced, one other ingredient is necessary – luck. It was the one ingredient which deserted me when I needed it most.

To support the argument that the England captaincy affected my form, much has been made of the fact that I scored centuries for England before I took over and immediately after I relinquished the job with none in between. But if you examine those centuries more closely you can see how big a part luck plays in success or failure at the crease, particularly the way I play.

In the second innings of the final Test against Australia in Melbourne during the 1979–80 tour I scored 119 in our eight-wicket defeat. The situation when I went in was very similar to the one at Headingley this summer. We were 88 for five in our second innings when I walked to the crease, still needing another 83 runs to avoid an innings defeat. That soon became 92 for six when Mike Brearley was out leaving me with the England tail. There was nothing to lose in having a go. I stayed to the end of our innings and took the score to 273 thanks to splendid support from Bob Taylor and John Lever who both hung around for long periods. Yet I should never have had the chance.

Fairly early in my innings Dennis Lillee attempted to bounce me and I went for the hook shot. I connected cleanly, controlled the stroke so that it did not go up in the air but hit it straight to Geoff Dymock at backward square leg. He should have taken the catch but put it down. Luck was on my side, a century the result.

Take a step forward in time to Trinidad and the first Test

against the West Indies in February 1981. I was captain by then and once again we were fighting to avoid an innings defeat on the last afternoon of the match. I had been at the wicket for 45 minutes when Clive Lloyd brought on my Somerset pal Viv Richards to bowl a few overs of off-spin and hurry along the new ball. There were a few fielders clustered around the bat and I thought I saw the opportunity to scatter them when Viv tossed up one delivery a little higher than usual.

I went for the drive, didn't quite get hold of it in my eagerness and skied the ball towards long on where Michael Holding needed to take just a couple of steps forward to take the catch which earned me universal condemnation from every Englishman on the ground. Yet I've no doubt I would have been acclaimed a hero if the ball had gone for six as I intended and the fielders had been spread out in a more defensive pattern.

Move forward in time again to the 1981 series against the Australians after I had lost the captaincy. I was very proud of many of the strokes I executed in scoring my centuries at Headingley and Old Trafford, but I will also be the first to admit that I got away with a few streaky ones on the Leeds wicket over and through the slips. The escape I remember most was at Old Trafford because it was the only mistake I made until I got out.

I was only just starting to strike out when I attempted to drive Terry Alderman back over his head. As in Trinidad, I didn't connect properly and skied the ball in the direction of long off. It meant a chase for Mike Whitney (playing in his first Test match) and an attempt to make an awkward catch with the ball dropping over his right shoulder. He got his fingertips to it but couldn't quite hold it. That was my bit of luck and it gave me another century against my name in the record books, my eighth in Test cricket.

You win some, you lose some. I won on those days in Melbourne and Manchester and I lost out in-between. Every player has his ups and downs, periods when everything seems to go right no matter how he plays, others when nothing runs for him. For three years before I assumed the captaincy everything had gone right for me and I was due for a bad patch. Even Sir Don Bradman had those. Geoff Boycott has, rightly, been acclaimed as England's most consistent batsman of the last fifteen years or so, but he went through a period in the mid-1970s when he opted out of Test cricket because things started going wrong for him. Unfortunately, my rough passage coincided with the captaincy. I'm convinced in my own mind that there was nothing more to it than that.

Except for my final Test as captain at Lord's, when the pressure of being on trial began to cloud my judgment and thoughts, I can honestly state that I did not feel an additional strain or burden when leading England. In fact I enjoyed it immensely. I made mistakes, of course. If I could go through it all over again I would change a number of things. Even in victory I've heard Mike Brearley say on a number of occasions that he would have played things differently, after he has looked back on the match and analysed his decisions.

Although I made mistakes I felt I was learning from every one. I felt, too, that I had learned the art of man management after what the England team had been through in the West Indies – the 'Robin Jackman Affair', the cancellation of the second scheduled Test in Guyana, a week of living out of a suitcase not knowing whether the tour was on or off and the tragic death of Ken Barrington during the Test match in Barbados which took away a man who had been a second father to me.

I felt, too, that I was just finding my form with the bat again when the 1981 Ashes series started. The second half of the tour to the Caribbean had been a disaster for me, run-wise, playing so little cricket and with little or no opportunity for practice in-between the games because of inadequate facilities. I was in bad nick and taking on Michael Holding and Co was not the best way of trying to play myself into form again.

At Trent Bridge, however, I felt it all coming back, particularly when I topscored with 33 in England's second innings. That is not many, I know, but only the player himself knows exactly how he feels and I felt right that day. The feeling was confirmed the following weekend when I scored 123 not out against Glamorgan at Swansea. I was back in the groove.

All I needed to go with it was the backing of the selectors, a chance of a run at the Australians by being appointed for at least three matches at a time and I'm sure everything would have worked out. It did work out all right for England, but not with me in charge. I regret that part of the most memorable cricketing summer for many years. But I was delighted for Mike Brearley and the part I played in helping him retain the Ashes. Putting personal disappointments aside, the most important issue was making England victorious again – especially against the Aussies.

2 First blow for the Australians

I didn't have the slightest hesitation in accepting when Alec Bedser, chairman of the England selectors, phoned me at Taunton on a Saturday evening towards the end of May and offered me the captaincy of England again for the three one-day games of the Prudential Trophy against Australia.

Before the West Indies tour had ended it seemed that almost all the critics had called for my head, insisting that there must be a change of leadership. Personally, I returned from the Caribbean with my head held high. We had lost the first two Test matches of that series – the first after rain had affected the start, which meant that we had had very little practice, the second when we were still trying to pull ourselves together again after the Robin Jackman rumpus and the shock of having to leave Guyana quickly.

We had had more than our fair share of difficulties – apart from the rain. The tour was perfectly planned from a West Indies point of view. Leaving aside Malcolm Marshall and Hartley Alleyne (of Hampshire and Worcestershire respectively) we had not come across a fast bowler until the famous West Indies foursome of Michael Holding, Andy Roberts, Colin Croft and Joel Garner was unleashed on us in the one-day international and the Test series. We had had no real practice against pace before the first Test and came across that fearsome foursome on one of the fastest wickets I'd experienced in the second Test in Barbados.

After a start like that we might easily have lost all four Test matches but we pulled ourselves together once the tour got on an even keel. The last two Test matches were saved and we returned with a great deal of our reputation and pride restored. I thought we had matured as a side as the tour progressed, with Graham Gooch, David Gower, Graham Dilley and John Emburey in particular finding themselves as true Test match players.

Perhaps the greatest mistake I made as England captain was to sound full of optimism in pre- or mid-match press conferences. Throughout the summer of 1980 at home against the West Indies I had always insisted that England were capable of winning the Test matches. And in the West Indies I kept the same theme going, although I realised that the odds were always stacked heavily against us. I was slaughtered by my critics for my 'heads will roll' comment on the rest day of the first Test in Trinidad. I had indicated that I thought we would save the game, although the match was only two days old and the West Indies were 365 for seven in their first innings. The comment became almost as famous as Tony Greig's 'we'll make them grovel' before the opening Test against the West Indies in England in 1976.

Perhaps I would have saved some comebacks if I had qualified my comments but I saw it as part of my duty as captain to encourage the team serving me as far as I could, especially when they had been continually written off. I was criticised for my comments but I don't think I would have won any supporters if I had stood up and said, 'We haven't got a price.'

Before the start of the first Prudential Trophy match at Lord's I was asked whether I thought it right that England should be favourites and whether England would take the three-match series. I said 'yes' to both questions. I wasn't trying to boost the team on that occasion: I honestly felt it was the case, although I know that playing a one-day game is something of a lottery. Somerset were favourites to take both the Benson and Hedges Cup and the new Nat West Bank Trophy during 1981 but we were beaten in the first round of the latter by Northants who were rated outsiders at that stage.

However, it was right that England were made favourites after the way we had beaten Australia in the two Prudential matches immediately before the Centenary Test at Lord's in 1980 when they had Greg Chappell leading them. He was missing in 1981 and that obviously robbed Kim Hughes's team of much of their batting power. They were going to miss him.

That phonecall from Alec Bedser offering me the England captaincy for the Prudential series had come when Somerset were in the middle of playing the Australians at Taunton. This enabled me to have a quick look at some of their players who were almost strangers to me, but unfortunately the rain robbed me of taking the hard look I really wanted. The rain had followed them around throughout their early programme, interrupting matches against Hampshire at Southampton, our match at Taunton, the next at Glamorgan and the following game against Gloucestershire at Bristol. They had spent more time sitting in the dressing-room than actually playing.

Coming from the sticky heat of Sri Lanka into the damp of England, they couldn't possibly be anywhere near their best with most of their batsmen having had only two visits to the crease. And most of those had been fairly brief introductions to English wicket conditions. If their batsmen had suffered, their bowlers were in a worse state. Dennis Lillee in particular had spent almost three weeks in hospital suffering from a chest virus and lost almost a stone in weight. Yet he was so vital to their cause that the Australian tour management willingly accepted his offer to play in the three-match series despite the fact he had been discharged from hospital only five days before the first Prudential game at Lord's. It was an extremely brave gesture by a fast bowler who had displayed tremendous courage throughout his career, especially in the way he had fought back to the top after a spine condition which would have forced many others to quit.

The Australians' lack of practice was one reason why I rated us as favourites. I also looked at the two teams man for man and came out with more pluses on the England side – a side largely made up of the players who had been with me in the West Indies plus two important additions in Yorkshire's Jim Love and Warwickshire wicketkeeper Geoff Humpage. The early season rain had also impeded our players but both these two had settled down very quickly and managed to make runs.

Love is another of the Yorkshire school who had always looked

---

Sometimes I win . . . sometimes I lose. If the ball is there to be hit I'll always have a go, whether it is a knockabout match or a Test game. That's the way I believe in playing cricket. When Terry Alderman overpitched during my century in the third Test at Headingley, I had no hesitation in driving him to the boundary for one of my twenty-six fours in my unbeaten 149

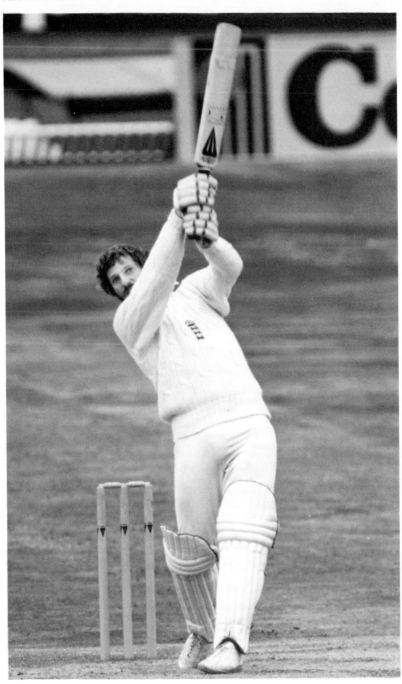

a good player, stylish and correct in the mould of Bill Athey, Neil Hartley, Richard Lumb and Kevin Sharp. All five have had their moments at the crease and it remains one of cricket's great mysteries why none has found the consistency to go with their class. At the start of the 1981 summer Love looked to have found that consistency and deserved his chance.

In limited-over cricket where fast or medium fast bowlers generally hold the key, it is not essential to select the country's best wicketkeeper. One who is competent standing back but is no slouch with the bat is often a safer bet and Humpage fitted that bill ideally. He had played a number of crucial limited-over innings in helping Warwickshire win the John Player League in 1980 and had struck form right from the off.

The rest of the side picked itself. Geoff Boycott, Graham Gooch, David Gower and Peter Willey had all scored Test match centuries in the West Indies. Mike Gatting had not, going through an unlucky period similar to mine when nothing went his way, yet he had still returned home a better player than when he started the tour. That improvement had shown itself in his early season form. With Graham Dilley struggling to adjust to English conditions again, I don't think there was any argument over the bowling make-up with Bob Willis, Robin Jackman and Mike Hendrick supporting me. The squad was completed by Derek Randall, who was included to act as a cover batsman and fielder extraordinary in case of injury, plus John Emburey if we came across a wicket at Lord's, Edgbaston or Headingley which we thought might encourage a spinner. We did not.

It was a sound enough squad which boosted my confidence and led me to predict victory for England in the series on the day before the opening match at Lord's. But, for the benefit of those who have said that I learned little during my year as England captain, I also made sure I covered my tracks this time. I warned everybody: 'At the same time it will not be easy. You can pick eleven guys off an Australian beach and they will give you a good game of cricket. An Australian side is never more dangerous than when it has been written off. It may have been described by Australian critics as the worst side to leave the country but nobody is selected to play for their country unless they are any good.'

That warning was conveniently forgotten when Australia came back to win the last two matches and take the trophy 2–1 and my pre-series prediction of victory was held against me. Just as I had warned, the Australians were at their most dangerous when they were down and apparently on the verge of being counted out after losing the opening match by six wickets. The way they came back was also a tribute to their captain Kim Hughes who showed himself to be a quick learner in the art of setting fields for limited-over cricket and the special demands of this type of cricket.

After playing Australia in the Benson and Hedges World Series on the 1979–80 tour when we beat them four times and again in the Prudential series before the Centenary Tests at home in 1980 when we won both games with considerable ease, I always felt that Greg Chappell was not particularly enamoured of limited-over cricket. For the most part he still insisted on setting orthodox fields as he would for a five-day Test match, seldom made allowances for the ingenuity of batsmen in finding ways to score where none exist and seemed unable to pick the right moment to change from attack to defence. Hughes was quick to pick up all these points after that first defeat.

The opening match went exactly as I expected. I put Australia in after winning the toss and was not dismayed by their 210 for seven off their 55 overs – a total inspired by an unbeaten 73 from their gritty left-handed batsman Allan Border who turned out to be their Man of the Test Series. I'm not forgetting the 42 wickets by Terry Alderman on his first overseas tour or the 39 collected by Lillee either.

After Bob Willis had struck with his second delivery in removing John Dyson leg-before, we were helped by two run-outs, the first to dismiss Graeme Wood, the second to send back Trevor Chappell (the latest in the line of Chappell brothers to represent Australia). With Wood's history of run-out mix-ups, which must better those of Geoff Boycott and even Denis Compton, there is always a chance of getting him or his partner that way. At Lord's it came in the ninth over when Chappell pushed Bob back down the wicket. There was never any chance of a run but Wood had committed himself and was left stranded by a couple of feet when Chappell rightly sent him back.

Next it was Chappell's turn and he could count himself unlucky. When I brought Robin Jackman into the attack Hughes drove fiercely at his first ball. From the moment the ball left the bat it looked a four all the way until Robin made a frantic dive to put himself in its path. It was a magnificent piece of athleticism, reaching the ball at the end of his follow-through. He had no other thought in his mind except to stop the ball but it bounced off his hands on to the wicket at the bowler's end before Chappell had a chance of getting home after backing up just a little too far.

My only worrying moments during the entire match came when Allan Border and Martin Kent got together in a 74 run partnership for the fifth wicket in 22 overs. Border had taken over after Chappell's run-out and Kent had come in when Hughes had fallen leg-before to Jackman with the score 60 for four after 20 overs. We had one opportunity to separate them when Kent gave a chance to David Gower in the covers off Jackman's bowling but otherwise they played well together.

Border was solid and secure, taking a six and a four off one wayward over from Willis, four boundaries in another from Graham Gooch. He was the dominant partner, drawing comfort from Kent's upright and elegant support at the other end. They had taken the score to 134 in the forty-second over before they were parted when Kent played a firm clip off his legs against me but aimed it straight to Gooch at mid-wicket. All that remained were a few clubbing blows from Border, Rod Marsh and Ray Bright before the innings ended. Their total of 210 for seven was respectable enough but never worrying on that Lord's wicket.

Graham Gooch was the batsman they feared most after the way he had taken them apart at Edgbaston the summer before in scoring 108 runs. They had good reason for he and Geoff Boycott gave us just the start we wanted, opening with an 86 run stand inside the first 27 overs. Of those runs Goochie took 53, sweeping

---

My bold approach doesn't always come off. Australia's left-arm spinner Ray Bright managed to get one past my bat during my second century in the fifth Test at Old Trafford, but I recovered quickly enough to prevent Rodney Marsh claiming his twelfth stumping during his remarkable ten-year reign behind the wicket

Bright into the Grandstand for one six, helping himself to half a dozen fours, and just ready to take the Australians apart again when he edged Lillee to first slip.

From that moment onwards it was very much a straightforward canter to victory apart from a minor hiccough or two. Despite his lack of practice and his illness, Lillee had been the pick of the Australian bowlers. However, on doctor's advice he was forced to bowl his eleven overs almost straight off to prevent him sweating up and then catching a chill waiting around in the outfield to come back as he would normally have done.

Goochie had fallen to the first ball of Lillee's tenth over, Mike Gatting went leg-before to the fourth ball of the same over, which meant that David Gower and Boycott had only eight more deliveries from Lillee to contend with before he disappeared into the pavilion for good.

With Lillee out of the way, the rest was comparatively easy. The third wicket partnership between Boycott and Gower was even more free than the opening stand. They added 86 together off 17 overs before Gower was caught at extra cover off an

Risky stroke this but I had no qualms about playing it, even though I was on 94 at the time. Bright had positioned Dennis Lillee on the boundary at Old Trafford to cut off the sweep stroke but there was nothing Lillee could do about this one as the ball went over his head for a six – and that was my century off only 86 deliveries

attempted drive. Jim Love stayed for 15 runs before being caught one-handed at slip by Ray Bright. We needed just another 12 runs for victory when I walked out. Boycott was on 75 and stayed on that total as I helped myself to all the runs we needed off the next over from Bright to secure our six-wicket victory with 3.2 overs to spare.

Our victory surprised nobody. It had been so emphatic that we were expected to win the next game two days later at Edgbaston. There was a call for Derek Randall to be included at number three, Mike Gatting would drop down the order to five and Jim Love be rested to make a re-appearance in the third match on his own Headingley ground. I didn't see it that way. It was true that

Mike Gatting was playing out of position at number three, which is Randall's normal spot in the Nottinghamshire side, and had failed with a duck at Lord's. For that very reason I thought he deserved another chance – and was glad in the end that he got it. Although Love had made only 15 at Lord's he had done nothing wrong and I believed it was best to stick with a winning side to make sure the trophy was won before doing any experimenting. It didn't turn out that way.

Worried about their batting failures at Lord's, the Australians decided to go for Graham Yallop's experience for the second game, moving Trevor Chappell up to opener in place of John Dyson. They also made room for Terry Alderman to step in by dropping Ray Bright whose 9.4 overs in the first match had gone for 43 runs.

Switching Yallop for Dyson proved to be a winner, even though Australia got off to a bad start when I again won the toss and put them in. In my first over I had Chappell caught behind on the leg side when he attempted to hook a bouncer which left them 10 for one. They recovered to score 249 for eight off their 55 overs, a healthy total. Yet it was one that I thought we should have bettered and indeed looked like doing so until a clatter of wickets right at the end of our innings in a moment of panic produced the first of the summer's surprising finishes. Only this one went against us.

A second wicket partnership of 86 between Wood and Yallop in 28 overs was the basis of what proved to be a winning Australian total. Mike Hendrick was as mean as ever in bowling his first seven overs for only eleven runs but Australia's second wicket pair made up for it by picking up runs against Goochie and Pete Willey. They were splitting the role of fifth bowler between them and I hoped to get them through their overs before the slog was on. Unfortunately it didn't quite work out that way as they conceded 74 runs between them off the eleven overs they shared.

Even so their rate of progress wasn't particularly inspired. They were scoring at only just over three an over when Bob Willis' finely-shaped nose appeared to cut a furrow in the Edgbaston outfield as he took a diving catch to dismiss Wood on the fine leg boundary. It was, in fact, a magnificent catch off a skier, the ball seemingly switching directions half a dozen times as it fell –

judging by Bob's antics in trying to get under it.

The rate picked up when Kim Hughes joined Yallop for a third wicket partnership which produced 64 runs in 15 overs before Yallop was bowled by Hendrick. Two superb run-outs then checked Australia, both coming off my bowling although I can't claim any credit. Hughes chanced his luck against Gower's arm when he pushed me into the covers and went for a single. He lost out by feet when the wicket was broken at my end. Then Allan Border took the same risk, playing me to Pete Willey at mid-off, and also perished. It needed a direct hit and Willey supplied it. It was left to Rodney Marsh and some robust hitting from Geoff Lawson to take Australia to their 249 for eight.

We needed to score at 4.5 an over but I was confident we could do it on that flat Edgbaston wicket. My confidence began to drain away before the innings was 16 overs old, by which time Goochie had been bowled by Rodney Hogg, Boycott had fallen to Geoff Lawson and Gower had been claimed by Terry Alderman. We were 36 for three and it could easily have been worse if Marsh had not had one of those days which earned him the nickname 'Iron Gloves' from the England players the first time they came across him in Australia back in 1970.

Gatting had made only two when he edged a ball from Alderman which Marsh would normally have swallowed with the greatest of ease. Down it went. Gatting had increased his total by only another eleven runs when he edged Alderman a second time. It was a real sitter this time, so easy that Marsh was a little too casual in his attempt to take it. Down it went again. Rod took it well when we kidded him after the match that about the only thing he had caught all day was one of those stupid streakers who had run on to the outfield. He evaded the attempts of the police to catch him but Rod brought him to the ground with a superb flying rugby tackle. He wasn't quite so happy when Mike Gatting called out 'thanks for the presents'. That Saturday was Mike's twenty-fourth birthday and he had almost won the match for us after his two escapes.

Mike had turned the match our way again when sharing in a 75 run partnership in 17 overs with Jim Love before the Yorkshire-man dragged on a delivery from Lawson. We were back in with a splendid chance when Pete Willey took over and helped Mike add

66 for the fifth wicket in 10 overs. It needed a superb catch by Wood in the covers to end Willey's innings. I know I am biased but I thought Hughes' catch at mid-on to dismiss me was equally brilliant, running around in circles to take one of those steepling skiers I've been known to hit from time to time.

It was disappointing but I wasn't too worried. Mike was in full stride. My seven-over stay with him had put on 47 runs. With five overs to go we needed only another 26 runs for victory with four wickets left and a batsman of Humpage's calibre walking to the crease. You'd always back the batting side in those circumstances, wouldn't you?

Unfortunately, we still had Dennis Lillee to contend with. Although he was never to be one hundred per cent fit throughout the summer, he was improving day by day after his period in hospital. Rain had caused a 65 minute stoppage in the morning but the afternoon turned out to be a beauty. There was no chill wind as there had been at Lord's which meant that Lillee did not have to be spared and Hughes could use him as his main strike bowler, bringing him back right at the death as is normal in limited-over cricket.

In his last but one over he removed Humpage. But victory still looked ours when Lillee began his last over with England needing six runs for victory – five if we did not lose a wicket – with three wickets left. Obviously Mike Gatting was our main hope having batted through 45 overs by then for his 96. Unfortunately he was at the wrong end. It was in an effort to give Mike the strike that Robin Jackman perished off the first ball of Lillee's last over when he attempted to sneak a single and was run out.

He sacrificed himself in getting Mike to the right end as we wanted but disaster followed. Mike took a mighty heave at the second ball of the over and connected superbly. At the worst it looked a four which would have given him his century. It might even have been a six which would have taken him into three figures and won the match. Instead it was neither. Standing two yards in from the long-off boundary was the figure of Lawson who made the catch look easy.

With our last pair at the wicket Willis and Hendrick still needed to find six runs with four balls left. Lillee's third ball produced a single for Willis, his fourth went for two leg-byes. With two

deliveries remaining and three runs wanted, Hendrick faced up to the fifth ball. He has a record of producing at least one straightish drive for four in his innings for England. He went for it this time, got a thin edge instead and Marsh made no mistake with the most vital chance of the day. Australia had squeezed home by just two runs.

Just how much the victory meant to them can be measured by the fact that when Kim Hughes walked into the players' dining-room for the after-match press conference, the Australian journalists rose to their feet and gave him a round of applause much to the astonishment of their English counterparts. That never happened to me. I know I never won a Test as captain, but I did lead England to victory in four limited-over internationals including one against the West Indies in 1980. I have to admit that the defeat was a shock to the system, something that had not entered into my calculations. I was glad then that I had added a rider to my pre-series predictions and warned of Australian capabilities when they are down. The summer of ups and downs, amazing turnarounds and Houdini-style escape acts had started. Australia's victory at least guaranteed that there would be no lack of interest in the third match at Headingley two days later.

It was too late for any experimenting now as far as England's side was concerned. All the batsmen had made runs in at least one of the two matches. There was no place for Randall and with the weather conditions at Leeds likely to help the faster bowlers, especially with a little cloud around, no place for Emburey's off-spin either. We kept the same side, Australia making one change with Dyson returning to open the innings, Chappell dropping back down the order to replace Kent. But the outcome of the match was not the only thing occupying the minds of the cricket-ing press or the selectors. The first Test match of the Ashes series at Trent Bridge was only eleven days away. England's first Test

---

The centuries at Headingley and Old Trafford belonged to happier days. I started the Ashes series disastrously by losing my middle stump at Trent Bridge when I drove over the top of a delivery from Alderman. I had made only one and Alderman was on his way to a record-breaking summer of 42 Test wickets in his first Test series

team was due to be picked five days after the match which meant finding a captain to make up the selection party.

My selection for the three-match Prudential series had been taken as a clear indication that I would get the position against Australia. The defeat at Edgbaston had put fresh doubt in the minds of many. Worse was to follow.

I completed a hat-trick of wins with the toss and put Australia in again as is normal in limited-over cricket. (Or rather Hughes lost the toss: as home captain my duty is to spin the coin and it's up to the visiting captain to make the call.) That was about the only thing that went England's way.

Graeme Wood was the villain as far as England were concerned. He dominated Australia's innings of 236 for eight by batting through 53 overs for 108 before being run out once again, attempting a second run when Love already had the ball in his hands at third man. His return was perfect. Perhaps he should not have been allowed to get that far, but he had already done enough damage in making 74 when we had our first chance of dismissing him. Gower made a superb stop in the covers when it seemed the ball had gone through and Wood was still trying to scamper home when the return was made. The swiftness of it all surprised Humpage as well. Neither he nor the ball arrived close enough to the wicket to effect the run-out. Wood had made only another three runs when Humpage had a second chance, a leg-side catch when the batsman flicked at Jackman but the ball failed to stick.

We did have one stroke of luck when Wood pushed Jackman gently back down the wicket and hared after a single. He got home safely enough but his partner Yallop had no chance as Jackman followed through to make the run-out. By then, however, Wood and Yallop had put on 130 for the second wicket in 28 overs and Australia were well on their way to their 236 even, although nobody else made any great contribution in their innings.

After losing Boycott to the fourth ball of Hogg's first over, Gooch and Gatting gave us hope with a 66 run partnership in 16 overs which kept us abreast of the required run rate. Then Gatting became the second victim of the Marsh–Hogg alliance and we drifted out of the picture. Although Australia bowled well in the conditions, our batting let us down. Where Marsh had dropped almost everything at Edgbaston, he caught all that moved at Headingley to finish with five catches. The runs flowed freely enough. So did the wickets. We needed a couple of batsmen to stand firm, slow it down a little so that we could regroup and rebuild. Willey attempted to do it but nobody settled down to stay with him. I was not any help either.

In the next eleven overs following Gatting's dismissal we made 62 runs, but also lost five wickets. With 18 overs to go we were heading for defeat on 133 for seven. There were still more than eight overs left when Hendrick became Marsh's fifth victim behind leaving Australia winners by 71 runs and Hughes to step forward to collect the Prudential Trophy plus a cheque for £5,000. We had to be content with £2,500 for our victory at Lord's. By then my own troubles had already started although I didn't know it at the time.

Throughout the day I had been conscious of a group of four people sitting huddled together from time to time on the pavilion balcony at Headingley just along from the England dressing-room. The group was made up of Alec Bedser and his fellow selectors Charlie Elliott, John Edrich and Brian Close. The topic under discussion was the England captaincy against Australia in the Test series.

I learned the outcome of their discussion soon after I had been dismissed for five. Alec Bedser called me aside and told me that they had decided to make me captain for the first match only and they would take stock of the situation after the first Test. Although I later told the cricket writers that I was happy with the situation and commented 'One Test is better than none', I was a little surprised and disappointed. I think the rest of the team were too when I told them. They offered their congratulations but they were not quite sure whether a word of sympathy might have been in order as well.

As the selectors had waited until England were losing the match before telling me the news I couldn't help wondering whether the defeat had any bearing on the one-match decision. But Alec announced at a press conference that their attitude would have been the same even if England had won handsomely. 'We are only doing what the Australians have done for years in home series,' he announced to the cricketing world. 'They never appoint a captain for a complete series but name him match by match after they have picked the team. It may bring extra pressure on Ian but playing in Test match cricket is all about pressure.'

The part about Test matches being all about coping with pressure was true. So was the part about Australia naming their captain match by match for their home series. With Somerset not having a match over the next three days I was able to spend a few days at home with my wife and two children, Liam and Sarah. They were happy, relaxing days, the last carefree days I was to spend with them for the next month, although I didn't know it at the time. Even then I couldn't help thinking of the one-match appointment and asking myself: 'Why the hell do England have to copy anything from Australian cricket?' I couldn't find a satisfactory answer.

Prudential Trophy scorecards

England v Australia at Lords, 4 June 1981
England won by six wickets

Australia			England		
J. Dyson	lbw Willis	2	G. A. Gooch	c Kent	
G. M. Wood	run out	22		b Lillee	53
T. Chappell	run out	16	G. Boycott	not out	75
K. J. Hughes	lbw Jackman	12	M. Gatting	lbw Lillee	0
A. R. Border	not out	73	D. I. Gower	c Kent	
M. Kent	c Gooch			b Chappell	47
	b Botham	28	J. Love	c Bright	
R. Marsh	b Botham	18		b Lawson	15
R. J. Bright	b Willis	18	I. T. Botham	not out	13
G. F. Lawson	not out	12	Extras		9
R. Hogg	} did not bat		Total (for 4 wkts) 212 (51.4 overs)		
D. K. Lillee					

Australia bowling		England bowling	
Extras	9	Hogg	11–1–36–0
Total (for 7 wkts) 210 (55 overs)		Lillee	11–3–23–2
		Lawson	9–0–51–1
Willis	11–0–56–2	Chappell	11–1–43–1
Botham	11–1–39–2	Bright	9.4–4–0–43–0
Hendrick	11–2–32–0		
Jackman	11–1–27–1	Fall of wicket: 1–86 2–86 3–172	
Willey	6–1–26–0	4–199	
Gooch	5–1–21–0		

Fall of wicket: 1–2 2–36 3–48 4–60
5–134 6–162 7–189

England v Australia at Edgbaston, 6 June 1981
Australia won by two runs

Australia			England		
G. M. Wood	c Willis		G. A. Gooch	b Hogg	11
	b Jackman	55	G. Boycott	b Lawson	14
T. Chappell	c Humpage		M. Gatting	c Lawson	
	b Botham	0		b Lillee	96
G. Yallop	b Hendrick	63	D. I. Gower	b Alderman	2
K. J. Hughes	run out	34	J. Love	b Lawson	43
A. R. Border	run out	17	P. Willey	c Wood	
R. Marsh	c Love			b Chappell	37
	b Botham	20	I. T. Botham	c Hughes	
M. Kent	lbw Willis	1		b Lawson	24
G. Lawson	not out	29	G. Humpage	b Lillee	5
D. K. Lillee	run out	8	R. Jackman	run out	2
R. Hogg	not out	0	R. Willis	not out	1
T. Alderman	did not bat		M. Hendrick	c Marsh	
				b Lillee	0
Extras		22			

Australia contd.

Total (for 8 wkts)	249 (55 overs)
Willis	11–3–41–1
Botham	11–1–44–2
Hendrick	11–2–21–1
Jackman	11–0–47–1
Willey	6–0–36–0
Gooch	5–0–38–0

Fall of wicket: 1–10 2–96 3–160
4–171 5–183 6–193 7–213 8–248

England contd.

Extras	12
Total	247 (54.5 overs)
Hogg	11–2–42–1
Lillee	10.5–2–36–3
Alderman	11–1–46–1
Lawson	11–2–47–3
Bright	—–0–69–1

Fall of wicket: 1–20 2–27 3–36
4–111 5–177 6–224 7–232 8–244
9–244

England v Australia at Headingley, 8 June 1981
Australia won by 71 runs

Australia

G. M. Wood	run out	108
J. Dyson	c Gooch b Hendrick	22
G. Yallop	run out	48
K. J. Hughes	c Gatting b Jackman	0
A. R. Border	c Jackman b Willis	5
R. Marsh	c Humpage b Botham	1
T. Chappell	c Gooch b Willis	14
G. Lawson	run out	8
D. K. Lillee	not out	0
R. Hogg T. Alderman	did not bat	
Extras		30
Total (for 8 wkts)		236 (55 overs)

Willis	11–1–35–2
Botham	11–2–42–1
Hendrick	11–2–31–1
Gooch	11–0–50–0
Jackman	11–1–48–1

Fall of wicket: 1–43 2–173 3–173
4–187 5–189 6–216 7–236 8–236

England

G. A. Gooch	c Marsh b Hogg	4
G. Boycott	c Marsh b Lawson	37
M. Gatting	c Marsh b Hogg	32
D. I. Gower	b Alderman	5
J. Love	b Chappell	3
P. Willey	c Marsh b Hogg	42
I. T. Botham	c Hughes b Chappell	5
G. Humpage	c Border b Alderman	6
R. Jackman	c Chappell	14
R. Willis	not out	2
M. Hendrick	c Marsh b Hogg	0
Extras		15
Total		165 (46.5 overs)

Hogg	8.5–1–29–4
Lillee	7–0–37–0
Lawson	11–3–34–1
Alderman	11–3–19–2
Chappell	9–0–31–3

Fall of wicket: 1–5 2–71 3–80 4–89
5–95 6–106 7–133 8–160 9–164

3 Opening Test tossed away
-first Test

I would number Trent Bridge in Nottingham among my favourite cricket grounds – if not top of the list. It was there on the last weekend of July 1976 that I made my maiden first-class century and came of age as a batsman at the ripe old age of 20. Under the watchful eye of Brian Close, Somerset's captain at the time, I went on to finish with an undefeated 167.

Exactly a year later I was back on the ground for another first, my debut for England under Mike Brearley's leadership against Greg Chappell's 1977 Australians. Pulling on that brand-new sweater with the three lions on the chest was thrilling enough but it was to get better when I finished the first innings with five wickets for 74 runs – the first of my 17 hauls of five or more wickets in a Test innings.

Yes, Trent Bridge is a ground for me to remember. But not for the happiest of reasons these days. I was back there in 1980 with England, leading my country for the first time, only to suffer a two-wicket defeat by the West Indies in a match we should have won if we had held our chances.

And it was exactly the same story in 1981. Seemingly one catch after another tossed aside and falling to earth to let the Australians off the hook when they should have been dead and buried by the end of their first innings. They were escapes which led to Australia's four-wicket victory inside four days, giving them a 1–0 lead in their bid to regain the Ashes. Only this time I was on trial as England's captain and the outside pressures were beginning to build up.

I couldn't have a go at the rest of the team over the dropped catches. Some observers counted as many as eight missed opportunities in the Australian first innings although that was taking it to ludicrous lengths. But there were certainly six which went to hand, five of them pretty straightforward and all in the arc between wicketkeeper and fourth slip. I couldn't complain because I was responsible for three of them going to ground.

Before the match started I had tried to forget that mine was a one-match appointment so I could tackle the game as if I were in charge for a complete campaign. It was a policy I adopted when I helped pick the team, looking at the summer as a whole in making my plans rather than just at the first Cornhill Test.

Humpage's appointment as wicketkeeper for the Prudential series had been strictly a limited-over move. For the Test matches we made wicketkeeping ability our first priority without taking batting potential into consideration. Alan Knott and Bob Taylor – still the best out and out wicketkeepers in the country in my opinion – were obviously considered but we took the future into account as well. This meant a place for Middlesex's Paul Downton, giving him his first home Test. He had improved considerably during the winter in the West Indies where he had been taken as second choice behind David Bairstow but finished up in command, producing a staunch match-saving performance with the bat to help David Gower draw the final Test in Kingston, Jamaica. He deserved another opportunity.

We made two other changes from the Prudential side. It was essential in the Test match to have one other batsman who was capable of playing a long innings to complement the stroke-makers such as Gower, Goochie and Gatting, three men who like to get a move on but who always offer the bowler a chance. We had tried three or four over the previous 12 months without any real success and decided to fall back on an experienced campaigner in Kent's Bob Woolmer.

Many found it an ironic choice. Bob had lost his Test place the previous summer largely because he had stayed around against the West Indies pace attack. Unfortunately he had not produced the weight of runs to go with his long spells at the crease. Against the Australian pace men we hoped he would be able to do both this time. The team was completed by Graham Dilley. I wanted him because he had the potential to be the fastest bowler on either side and had done all that I asked of him in the Caribbean. John Emburey was also in the party but one look at the wicket on the Thursday morning was enough to make him the spare man. The

Australians came to the same conclusion because they left out left-arm spinner Ray Bright from their 12 and opted for a four-man pace attack.

With Clive Rice and Richard Hadlee in the Nottinghamshire side, they were making their wickets green and bouncy at Trent Bridge to aid their championship ambitions. The Test pitch was no exception. It was nippy too, as well as offering considerable lateral movement under cloudy skies. Unfortunately the bounce was not as regular as it should have been. This was not an ideal Test wicket. It was like asking Steve Davis and Hurricane Higgins to play a world championship match on a snooker table that produced bouncy cushions like a pin-ball machine in an amusement arcade. The wicket was biased too much in favour of the bowlers. The cricket it produced, however, was spectacular and entertaining. The batsmen may not have liked it but the crowd certainly did.

I knew what to expect when Kim called right for a change; he didn't need to tell me that he was putting us in. In just over four hours we were bowled out for 185. Yet I finished the day well satisfied with our position when Australia were reduced to 33 for four in reply.

Lillee blasted away the foundation of our innings with a magnificent opening spell in which he hardly wasted a delivery and collected the wickets of Goochie and Woolmer. He made the batsmen play at almost every delivery and Goochie had little chance against one which bounced a little higher than most, left him, found the edge and Wood did the rest at first slip. That was in Lillee's third over. In his next he produced another which rose sharply, caught the shoulder of Woolmer's bat and Wood took another first slip catch, this time high above his head. We were 13 for two and in trouble.

Alderman was the next to strike. He claimed his first Test wicket when he had Boycott checking his stroke but not quickly enough to get his bat out of the way, leaving Border to take a fine diving catch at second slip. The wicket fell just when it appeared that Boycott and Gower were beginning to put us on top. Boycott had been in trouble several times but put each alarm behind him, whilst Gower was playing easily and relaxed. He has such a keen eye that he appears to have more time than any other batsman to cope with the fastest of bowling. It also tends to give him a false sense of security.

Gower has always had a liking for picking up runs through the gully region – so much so that many county sides automatically place two gullies when they see him walking to the wicket. Hughes did the same and was rewarded when Lillee returned for his second spell. Gower attempted to cut a ball that was a little too close to him and Yallop, the first of the two gullies, held the catch. After the way he had been playing his loss was a tragic one as far as England's cause was concerned. We were then four down for 67 and two more wickets were to fall before we reached three figures. One of them was mine.

Willey went first, soon after lunch, when giving Border his second slip catch, and I made only one before playing across a yorker from Alderman which took my middle stump. The same bowler was to claim the next wicket, that of Downton, which gave him three in a row towards the end of his 24 over spell into the wind. It was an impressive debut for a youngster who had started the day bowling too short but gradually learned to pitch the ball up, forcing the batsmen to come forward and giving them less chance to counter the lateral movement he was obtaining from the wicket.

We were then 116 for seven. The fact that we managed to climb towards respectability on 185 was entirely down to Gatting and Dilley. Mike played extremely well, firm off his legs, fierce square of the wicket on the offside whenever the bowlers dropped short and showing keen judgment when picking the delivery to leave alone in making his half century.

Dilley was never so circumspect. His was a good, old-fashioned 'blood and thunder' innings of the type they tell me fast bowlers used to produce many years ago. The ball didn't always go where he intended during his 43 run eighth wicket partnership with Gatting, but the Australian bowlers and fielders were more surprised than Dill was.

Finding a partner to stay with him at last, Gatting obviously thought he would be at the wicket for a good few overs. He signalled his confidence by waving to John Emburey to take out another pair of batting gloves when he attempted a pull against Hogg and was leg-before to one which kept low. Bob Willis went first ball to a leg-side catch, but nothing troubled Dilley who went merrily on carving up the bowling to double his score during a last wicket partnership of 26 before he waved the bat once too often and was bowled.

The Australian pace attack had used the wicket well, and their fielders had given splendid support. Seven catches were offered, seven catches were taken between first slip and gully which gives an indication of how much the ball was moving off the pitch. We were to use the conditions even better, but sadly our fielders let the bowlers down. I've already admitted to being the main culprit.

Our position demanded a devastating reply that night. Willis, Dilley and Hendrick supplied it. I told them all before we went out: 'The conditions were hard enough for us, it's going to be even worse for them.' So it proved.

Their innings was only two balls old when Wood was out leg-before to Dilley. How Yallop survived the next four balls I shall never know. Dyson should not have survived Willis' second over but he escaped when I put down the first of the catches at second slip. It did not prove too costly in terms of runs with Dyson making only five, but those runs occupied him for fifty minutes. If I had accepted the chance we might have had five or six wickets down that first evening instead of four.

Willis was the man to get rid of Dyson. I switched him to take over from Dilley so that he would have the benefit of the wind for his second spell. The Australian opener tried to fend off a delivery which bounced chest-high only to drop it into the hands of Woolmer at short leg. Without addition to the score the extra bounce accounted for Yallop when he played on trying to control a delivery from Hendrick. Willis completed a marvellous comeback in the final over of the day when he had Hughes leg-before. I was the one wearing a smile when I walked into the Australian dressing-room for a quick beer that evening.

Australia should never have made 100 but we allowed them to get within six runs of our first innings total which was to prove decisive in the end. We spilled five catches on that second day, including two offered by the main Australian dangerman, Border, when he had made 10 and 17 respectively. He went on to hold the innings together with a top-scoring 63. Even now, I can't explain our failings when the Australians pouched everything.

The first chance Border offered was perhaps the easiest of the lot, straightforward, waist-high to Downton. So easy that he attempted to catch it and throw it up in the air in delight in the same movement. His delight turned to misery when it popped out again. The next one Border offered came to me, a couple of feet above my head at second slip. I saw it leave the bat, went up for it and was on my way down again when the ball clipped my finger-tips. It had come off the bat slower than I had expected. The same thing happened to Dilley later in the day soon after Lillee had gone to the crease. He closed his hands before the ball reached him.

Whatever the reasons for our fumblings, the result proved catastrophic. Although we didn't bowl quite as well as we had done on the first evening, I suppose, looking back, we still took wickets regularly enough. The highest partnership for the Australians was achieved when Lillee joined Border, survived that chance to Dilley off me and stayed around while 37 were put on for the eighth wicket. Before then Border had put on 31 with Trevor Chappell, another 25 with Marsh – the wicketkeeper scoring 19 of them with some bludgeoning blows – and 21 with Lawson. Later he was to add 26 with last man Alderman before driving the ball back firmly in my direction, the one catch I was able to hold.

His was a particularly brave innings, the forerunner of several others he was to play in the series. The conditions were no easier than they had been on the first day. In addition he had to contend with some murky periods of light and drizzle which produced an unsatisfactory stop-start day. It is always felt that batsmen suffer most when players are continually forced off the field due to bad light or rain which means they have to play themselves in all over again when the game restarts. Yet bowlers suffer just as much. Every bowler likes to get into a rhythm before he feels completely at ease. With some bowlers it takes three or four deliveries, and with others it may take an over or two. Rain interruptions destroy the rhythm of a bowler as much as they upset the concentration of the batsmen. Even worse, the bowler has to contend with a wet ball.

Because of the rain and bad light the Australian innings, which started on the first evening, wasn't brought to an end until the third morning. Hughes was doing the smiling now. His side had scored 90 runs more than even he expected. Soon his smile was even broader. By the time we had extended our six-run first innings advantage to 19, we had lost Goochie, Boycott and Woolmer a second time around, two of them falling to brilliant catches.

With our score on 12 Yallop had taken off in the gully to cling to a superbly struck cut by Goochie off Lillee. At the same total Boycott had edged a catch behind pushing forward against Alderman but beaten off the wicket. Only one more had been added when Marsh dived full length to his right to take a one-handed catch leaving Woolmer – the man we had brought back to play a long innings – nursing a pair on his Test comeback.

This alarming slump was followed by two leg-before decisions dismissing Gatting and Willey so that by the time I went out to bat we were only 67 runs ahead. I lasted 65 minutes – enough to take the England innings into the fourth day, as well as convince myself that my batting touch was returning. Gower was again playing soundly. There still seemed a great chance of repairing the damage if we could see out the day. Sadly the gully region proved fatal for Gower once more just before the close, by which time we were exactly 100 runs on with only four wickets left.

The odds were still greatly stacked in Australia's favour when we returned for a historic fourth day. It was the first time Test cricket had been played on a Sunday in England. Yet I had not given up all hope. Although the weather had improved and the wicket was playing a little easier, I felt we still had a chance of pulling off my first Test victory as captain if we could have set Australia 150 plus to chase in their second innings. Looking back I'm sure I would have been proved right.

Unfortunately, we managed to set them only 132 to win, our last four wickets going down in 50 minutes on the fourth morning for the addition of 31 runs. I made another ten of them before edging a ball to second slip, but had the satisfaction of finishing top scorer and came off with my confidence bolstered as far as my personal fortunes were concerned. I hadn't felt so comfortable with a bat in my hand in Test matches for 12 months and I had been pleased with my bowling too, having swung the ball more in my old style.

If it had been essential to strike quickly at the start of Australia's first innings, it was even more vital when they went out to begin their second. But we didn't manage to strike quite quickly enough to cause the panic which ruined their two victory bids at Headingley or Edgbaston, nor did we have the same kind of good fortune.

In his anxiety to blast an early inroad into the Australian innings, Dilley was a little too wayward in his opening spell. He bowled slightly too short and too wide which allowed both Wood and Dyson to settle down without having to play at many deliveries when I wanted to force them to play, hoping they would make an error of judgment before they had adjusted to the conditions. Wood did in the end, turning Willis into the hands of Woolmer at short leg when the Australians had made 20. Dyson might have gone the same way soon after when he played me uppishly on the leg-side offering a sharp chance that Woolmer couldn't grasp. They had doubled the score by the time Gatting hurled himself full length at second slip and got two hands to an edge from Yallop against me.

That was 40 for two. I was convinced it was 40 for three a couple of balls later. Kim Hughes drove at me and I thought I detected a thin edge and saw the ball deviate the moment it went past the bat. I went up in my appeal immediately. So did wicket-keeper Downton and the slips, but umpire Bill Alley didn't move a muscle. I was still angry when I snatched my sweater away from him at the end of the over. The score had crept up to 77 for two when I turned to Dilley again. He produced the spell of the match which so nearly brought about the miracle we needed at the time.

Brian Clough, the Nottingham Forest manager, likes his cricket: he popped into Trent Bridge several times during the first Test, but was missing when I did my party piece. *Opposite above:* There was no time to bend down and pick up the ball when Allan Border went for a quick single against my bowling. *Middle:* The situation called for some of the fancy footwork I'd picked up as a Scunthorpe United reserve striker in an attempt at a run-out. *Below:* Unfortunately my finishing proved as wayward as the finishing of England's football side. My final shot was wide of the stumps

Miracles, it seems, are the exclusive right of Mike Brearley when he is England captain.

With his first ball back Dilley had Hughes leg-before. In his second over back, he had Dyson caught behind. Australia were 80 for four, still 52 runs away from safety. Then Chappell and Border dug in with a 42 run partnership before Dilley was able to strike again. It was too late. He threw one final scare into the Australian innings when he brought one back to bowl Border between bat and pad and then, two balls later, dismissed Marsh leg-before. Lawson joined Chappell to make sure there were no more mishaps.

So we were 0–1 down at the start of the Ashes campaign. But, with five more matches to go in the first six-match Test series in England, I wasn't as downhearted as many people had imagined I would be.

The confidence of the Australians had obviously increased dramatically following their Prudential Trophy success. Victory in the opening Cornhill match would now make them even harder to beat. Yet I still thought we were the better side man for man. We had lost because we dropped our catches and they held the ones that went their way. If we had done the same it would have been no contest. There was no reason why we should not get back into the series. I was confident that the Ashes would still be in England's care at the end of the summer. I was not so confident that I would be given the chance to retain them.

Just as I had been conscious of the selectors meeting on the balcony at Headingley during the last Prudential Trophy match, I was well aware that there had been considerable activity on the Sunday at Trent Bridge along the rabbit warren of corridors at the back of the Nottinghamshire pavilion. With the team for the second Test to be picked on the following Friday I reasoned – along with everybody else – that the selectors would let me know my fate before I left the ground that evening. I assumed that if I was allowed to drive away without them having spoken to me then I was a certainty for the chop.

Nothing was said to me in the morning, before the match started. Nothing was said at lunch. There was still no word at tea. No immediate response either when I walked off the field at the end. Then, just when it seemed I was to be left in the dark, Alec

England v. Australia
at Trent Bridge, Nottingham
18th, 19th, 20th, 21st and 22nd June, 1981

ENGLAND

#	Batsman		1st		2nd
1	G. Boycott	ct Border bld Alderman	27	ct Marsh bld Alderman	4
2	G. A. Gooch	ct Wood bld Lillee	10	ct Yallop bld Lillee	6
3	R. A. Woolmer	ct Wood bld Lillee	0	ct Marsh bld Alderman	0
4	D. I. Gower	ct Yallop bld Lillee	26	ct Sub bld Lillee	28
5	M. W. Gatting	lbw Hogg	52	lbw Alderman	15
6	P. Willey	ct Border bld Alderman	10	lbw Lillee	13
7	I. T. Botham (Capt.)	bowled Alderman	1	ct Border bld Lillee	33
8	P. R. Downton (Wkt.)	ct Yallop bld Alderman	8	lbw Alderman	3
9	G. R. Dilley	bowled Hogg	34	ct Marsh bld Alderman	13
10	R. G. D. Willis	ct Marsh bld Hogg	0	ct Chappell bld Lillee	1
11	M. Hendrick	not out	6	not out	0

Byes — Wides 1 — Leg Byes 6 — No Balls 4 — Extras 11 — **TOTAL 185**

Byes — Wides — Leg Byes 8 — No Balls 1 — Extras 9 — **TOTAL 125**

Wkts.	1	2	3	4	5	6	7	8	9	10
Fell	13	13	57	67	92	96	116	159	159	185

Wkts.	1	2	3	4	5	6	7	8	9	10
Fell	12	12	13	39	61	94	109	113	125	125

AUSTRALIA

#	Batsman		1st		2nd
1	G. M. Wood	lbw Dilley	0	ct Woolmer bld Willis	8
2	J. Dyson	ct Woolmer bld Willis	5	ct Dowton bld Dilley	38
3	T. M. Chappell	bowled Hendrick	17	not out	20
4	K. J. Hughes (Capt.)	lbw Willis	7	lbw Dilley	22
5	A. R. Border	ct and bowled Botham	63	bowled Dilley	20
6	G. N. Yallop	bowled Hendrick	13	ct Gatting bld Botham	6
7	R. W. Marsh (Wkt.)	ct Boycott bld Willis	19	lbw Dilley	0
8	G. F. Lawson	ct Gower bld Botham	14	not out	5
9	D. K. Lillee	ct Downton bld Dilley	12		
10	R. M. Hogg	ct Boycott bld Dilley	0		
11	T. M. Alderman	not out	12		

Byes 4 — Wides 1 — Leg Byes 8 — No Balls 4 — Extras 17 — **TOTAL 179**

Byes 1 — Wides — Leg Byes 6 — No Balls 6 — Extras 13 — **TOTAL for 6 wkts 132**

Wkts.	1	2	3	4	5	6	7	8	9	10
Fell	0	21	21	33	64	89	110	147	153	179

Wkts.	1	2	3	4	5	6	7	8	9	10
Fell	20	40	77	80	122	122				

ENGLAND	O	M	R	WK	N	W	O	M	R	WK	N	W
LILLEE	13	3	34	3		1	16.4	2	46	5		
ALDERMAN	24	7	68	4	1		19	3	62	5		
HOGG	11.4	1	47	3	3		3	1	8		1	
LAWSON	8	3	25									

AUSTRALIA	O	M	R	WK	N	W	O	M	R	WK	N	W
DILLEY	20	7	38	3	2		11.1	4	24	4	1	
WILLIS	30	14	47	3	2		13	2	28	1	5	
HENDRICK	20	7	43	2			20	7	33			
BOTHAM	16.5	6	34	2		1	10	1	34	1		

Umpires: W. E. Alley & D. J. Constant   Scorers: W. R. Thornley & D. K. Sherwood

Australia won by 4 wickets

Bedser filled the doorway to the dressing-room, took me on one side and said, 'We've decided to give you the next match at Lord's.'

My mind was still too cluttered up with the match for the real implications to sink in. I can remember I was just slumped on the bench in the corner of the dressing-room when the cricket writers found me. I could only repeat what I had said at Headingley: 'At least it's better than nothing,' I told them. They all appeared embarrassed, undecided whether to say a polite 'congratulations' or not. In fact the whole atmosphere in the dressing-room was one of embarrassment as the rest of the players quickly changed, packed and set off on their separate ways.

4 The agony of my Lord's trial -second Test

Throughout the Test at Trent Bridge I had tried to approach the match as though I was in charge for the entire summer but had been constantly reminded that I was in a one-off situation. I am not a great newspaper reader when it comes to cricket reports but there are always numerous newspapers lying around the dressing-room, and it is impossible not to take in the headlines. Whenever I switched on the radio or television set in my hotel room it seemed only a matter of seconds before the Test match was mentioned and millions of listeners were reminded yet again that I had been appointed for one match and was 'on trial'.

The situation became worse as the match progressed. It had started badly with reports that Bob Willis had attacked my appointment as captain for the Trent Bridge Test in a local radio interview, and this in turn had stirred up stories about dressing-room unrest. In fact Bob had been discussing a recent book he had written and did offer the opinion that he thought I had been given the captaincy too early when appointed against the West Indies a year before. What appeared in print – sent to the newspapers by the local radio station – had been taken completely out of context. Even so Bob was later fined by the Test and County Cricket Board.

Bob is entitled to his opinion. It didn't worry me. And it certainly didn't cause any ill-feeling or signal any unrest in the dressing-room. When we reported to Trent Bridge on the Wednesday before the Test match for a lunch and practice session, we chose pegs side by side in a corner of the dressing-room. He may have had reservations about my captaincy ability but there is no greater trier to have in your side.

By the end of the match some of the stories that appeared were just plainly ridiculous. It had upset me that each day's play was

not analysed to reflect the fortunes of the game but whether it
increased or decreased my chances of being appointed captain for
the next Test. After the first day's play one newspaper carried a
report saying that the most significant cricket happening had
taken place not at Trent Bridge but at Ilford where Keith Fletcher
had scored a century against Middlesex. Mike Gatting's courageous 52, perhaps his finest Test match innings at that stage of his
career, scarcely got a mention yet it deserved the headlines. On
the Saturday of Trent Bridge Mike Brearley turned up to write a
comment piece for the *Sunday Times* on the day's play, Middlesex
not being engaged in a county championship match. There was
nothing sinister about his appearance on the ground yet that was
interpreted as a move to have Mike reinstated.

It was to get worse. The day after I had been appointed to lead
England at Lord's, a story appeared saying that the selectors had
actually sacked me on the Sunday morning but changed their
minds later in the day. That was a completely fabricated story.
Alec Bedser was furious when he was told about it and made an
immediate protest to the Test and County Cricket Board who, in
turn, protested to the newspaper concerned. However, by then
the damage had already been done, the readers of the sports
pages believing I had been sacked.

It was against this background of rumour and speculation that I
had to lead England into the second Test seeking a victory which
would level the series. In an effort to achieve this we made one
change in the England 12 and two in the actual team. Apart from
dropping that one catch off Border, Downton had not looked
entirely happy behind the wicket in the first Test. His hands were
not working together and he had dropped too many deliveries
which came straight through to him. That meant another chance
for Bob Taylor and a memorable period for him.

While England had been engaged at Trent Bridge, Bob had
been making his maiden first-class century after 20 years of
trying. He was also on the verge of his fortieth birthday and of
breaking John Murray's world record of 1,270 catches. I had been
a party to dropping him 12 months before, just after he had set a
record of 10 dismissals in a Test match playing against India in the
Jubilee Test in Bombay on our way home from Australia. Eight of
those catches had been taken off my bowling, helping me to

become the only player to score a century and take 10 or more wickets in the same Test. Bob had also shared in a 171 run partnership with me. It was good to have him back.

As usual, the Lord's wicket had been stripped of any grass which meant a place for John Emburey's off-spin rather than Mike Hendrick's medium pace. The Australians made one change with Bright taking over from the injured Hogg who had been ruled out with a back injury. I gather he would have lost his place anyway.

At the start of the match, for a brief moment, the spotlight was taken off me and transferred to Geoff Boycott who was making his one hundredth Test appearance. Fittingly it was to be at the game's headquarters. Knowing Geoff's great sense of occasion there was considerable speculation as to whether he could score the 184 runs he needed to overtake Colin Cowdrey's aggregate of 7,624 Test runs and become the highest-scoring Englishman in Test history. After all, he had shown superb timing in scoring his one hundredth first-class century in front of his beloved fellow Yorkshiremen at Leeds in 1977 when facing Australia in a Test. If Cowdrey's record was not to go, he would dearly have loved a century to mark the occasion.

The only 100 he achieved was in staying at the crease for exactly 100 minutes on the first morning over a cautious 17 runs when Hughes again called correctly and put us in. His decision surprised me. I don't think I would have taken the same one but Hughes reckoned the wicket could only improve and there would be more in it for his fast bowlers on the first morning, especially with a little low cloud around.

The way that Goochie hammered 44 of the first 60 runs must have made Hughes wince. It was Lords 1980 all over again when he took that splendid century off the West Indies, his first in Test cricket. Lillee felt the brunt of it, his first seven overs costing 35 runs. He was forced out of the attack, which proved a stroke of good luck for the Australians. Lawson, younger and faster, took over and in his second over had Goochie mishooking to square leg against a delivery which came on him a little faster than he anticipated.

Our troubles were just beginning. No sooner had Woolmer arrived at the wicket than he received a painful blow from Lawson on his left forearm which deadened a nerve. He watched Boycott fall to a slip catch off Lawson before retiring hurt in considerable pain and rushing off to hospital to see if there was any fracture. With interruptions for rain and bad light, Gower never settled down and became Lawson's third victim when offering a chance behind. Bright accounted for Gatting just before the close. But not before Gatting had scored his second half-century of the series, batting with the assurance he had demonstrated in the first Test. We were 191 for four at the close, neither side having established an advantage.

The first part of the second day belonged to us when Peter Willey and nightwatchman John Emburey put on 97 together for the fifth wicket. Willey was the first out after scoring 82 runs. He displayed the guts and character he had shown in the West Indies when he had faced up to the fast bowlers by getting into line whatever they sent down in his direction. That was the start of our slide. Our last six wickets went down for the addition of only 27 runs, including mine when I was adjudged leg-before against Lawson without scoring. I didn't think much of the decision.

The day ended with another unsightly scene at Lord's, the second successive Test on the ground where there had been trouble. Enough time had been lost during the day to send the match into the extra hour with Australia having started their first innings in reply to our 311. By seven o'clock the skies had darkened again. Umpires Don Oslear and Kenny Palmer offered the light to the Australian openers who, quite understandably in the circumstances, decided to go off. As I left the field I checked the situation with the umpires and said, 'That's it for the day then, isn't it?' They agreed. When I got back to the dressing-room I told the lads it was shower-time.

I had always understood that when we came off for bad light or rain during the extra hour, play was automatically suspended for the day. So did everybody else I spoke to. Usually it doesn't matter because the light seldom improves after seven at night. Unfortunately, on this occasion the ground was soon bathed in sunlight again, fit enough for play. By this time most of the players were either having a shower or drying off afterwards. There was no chance of getting ready again and out in time to bowl another over before 7.30. But there was certainly no question of us not *wanting* to play – an accusation levelled at both Greg Chappell and myself during the Centenary Test ten months earlier when failure to cover a used wicket on the edge of the square during torrential rain made a large area of the outfield dangerous. I would have seized any chance of starting again in the hope of grabbing one or more Australian wickets.

With the crowd having been told over the loudspeaker system that play could continue right up until 7.30, a section demonstrated their disapproval when this decision was reversed by hurling seat cushions on to the outfield. Several hundred must have been thrown, and not all by angry spectators. Friends told me later that quite a few were hurled from the Warner Stand which is reserved for MCC members and their guests. After a day when the wine flowed quite freely, especially during the earlier hold-ups in play, several challenges were issued to see who could throw a seat cushion the furthest!

It was a scene cricket could have done without; angry voices were raised once again along the corridors of the Lord's pavilion. If the umpires got it wrong, they have my sympathy. With all the various competitions we have in cricket today, each with its own variation of the regulations, life can be very confusing. The day must surely come when one man is put in charge of the Test matches and has the power to take instant decisions and relieve the umpires of some of the burden they have to carry. At the moment the ground authority is technically in charge which means five different masters in a six Test match season. Surely it would make sense if the Test and County Cricket Board were in complete control and ran each Test match?

The third day, like the second, saw us in charge for the first half before letting the advantage slip. Wood seemed determined to prove that anything Goochie could do he could do better. He raced along to make 44 out of the first 62 scored before Taylor celebrated his return behind the wickets with a diving one-handed catch. It was the start of a mini-slump which saw Dyson, Yallop and Chappell out by the time the score had advanced to 81. That is when Border came in and took charge. He and Hughes took the score to 167 before the Australian captain was well caught by Willis at mid-off. Border stayed until they were in sight of our total at 244 before he steered me to second slip.

My hopes of a first innings lead, however slender, vanished on the Monday morning when Marsh, Bright and then Lillee indulged themselves. All three played and missed on several occasions, especially against Willis who did well to get to the wicket and bowl. He had spent the Sunday rest day in bed with a chest infection and I know more than one bowler who would not have made it to the ground.

The result of it all was that instead of the useful lead I had envisaged when Australia were 81 for four, Australia crept 34 runs ahead. That still didn't stop me thinking in terms of victory, with Australia having to bat last and the chance that the wicket might be of some assistance to Emburey.

But the first prerequisite was to make sure we worked our way into a position whereby we couldn't lose. Boycott and Gower virtually made certain of that with a stand of 123 for the third wicket in 194 minutes. Goochie had gone when we were still 3 runs in arrears, Woolmer when were were only 21 runs ahead, but Boycott batted without the slightest sign of discomfort while Gower got his head down, remembered his footwork and cut out the dainty stuff which has often proved his downfall when looking good. He couldn't afford to take any chances of being troubled by the rough outside the offstump to a left-hander.

By mid-morning on the final day we were virtually in the clear and needed to chase runs quickly if we were to have any hope of bowling Australia out a second time. The early progress had not been as swift as I had hoped. Boycott had been 47 not out overnight and needed another 41 minutes to score the additional three runs for his half-century. When he was eventually out, caught behind attempting to steer a ball through the slip area, I had to ask the other batsmen to go for their shots from the off, which they willingly did.

In such circumstances there are bound to be some mishaps. Ours occurred when three wickets went down with the score on 217. They included mine when I attempted to sweep the first ball I received from Bright against the spin and was bowled. I had bagged a pair.

Gower and Gatting had previously gone at the same score. When I walked out to the wicket I had already made up my mind that if Bright gave me one to sweep I would have a go. He did and

I missed. Bagging a 'pair' in a Test match at Lord's didn't bother me. I had played that stroke simply because we were chasing runs and the risk seemed worthwhile. I felt no shame, no thought of having disgraced myself or of having let the side down in any shape or form. At that particular stage of the match my failure didn't matter. I would never have guessed it looking at the faces of the MCC members as I walked back into the completely silent pavilion.

I was made to feel like a villain as I approached the members sitting in their seats in front of the pavilion. Most of them sat unmoving, staring straight ahead, seemingly doing their best to ignore me completely. A few others glanced in my direction as I approached the gate and started to climb the steps, but none of them would look me in the eye. Whenever I looked up or about me, eyes were quickly averted. By then I had already made up my mind to quit the captaincy if the selectors were going to prolong my match-by-match examination. If my mind hadn't been made up, I'm sure the attitude of the MCC members that day would have made it up for me.

In the first hour after lunch we added 68 runs off 16 overs enabling me to declare, setting the Australians to make 232 to win in 170 minutes which might have tempted them if they had made a reasonable start. Although the odd ball was turning, the wicket was flat and I really needed to keep the Australians interested in victory to stand a reasonable chance of bowling them out. As it turned out we were probably too successful for our own good.

In the second over of the innings Dyson fell leg-before against Dilley for a duck. In the ninth Yallop edged a catch to me off Willis. In the fifteenth Dilley had Hughes leg-before whereupon Chappell came in and dropped anchor. The Australians appreciated that Emburey presented the greatest danger and treated him accordingly so that the 21 overs he got through cost him only 24 runs. Even then I didn't abandon hope until the last possible moment. There were only 13 balls remaining when I finally called off the hunt, having succeeded in taking just one more wicket, that of Chappell.

By then I was thoroughly and utterly cheesed off. There were still the Cornhill after-match awards to wade through before I

Match Drawn

LORD'S ⟨MCC⟩ GROUND

CORNHILL INSURANCE TEST SERIES
ENGLAND v. AUSTRALIA

THURS., FRI., SAT., MON. & TUES., JULY 2, 3, 4, 6 & 7, 1981   (5-day Match)

ENGLAND

			First Innings		Second Innings	
1	G. A. Gooch	Essex	c Yallop b Lawson	44	l b w b Lawson	20
2	G. Boycott	Yorkshire	c Alderman b Lawson	17	c Marsh b Lillee	60
3	R. A. Woolmer	Kent	c Marsh b Lawson	21	l b w b Alderman	9
4	D. I. Gower	Leicestershire	c Marsh b Lawson	27	c Alderman b Lillee	89
5	M. W. Gatting	Middlesex	l b w b Bright	59	c Wood b Bright	16
6	P. Willey	Northamptonshire	c Border b Alderman	82	c Chappell b Bright	12
7	J. E. Emburey	Middlesex	run out	31		
†8	I. T. Botham	Somerset	l b w b Lawson	0	b Bright	0
*9	R. W. Taylor	Derbyshire	c Hughes b Lawson	0	b Lillee	9
10	G. R. Dilley	Kent	not out	7	not out	27
11	R. G. D. Willis	Warwickshire	c Wood b Lawson	5	Innings closed	
			B 2, l-b 3, w 3, n-b 10,	18	B 2, l-b 8, w , n-b 13,	23
			Total	311	Total	265

FALL OF THE WICKETS

1—60 2—65 3—134 4—187 5—284 6—293 7—293 8—293 9—298 10—311
1—31 2—55 3—178 4—217 5—217 6—217 7—242 8—265 9— 10—

ANALYSIS OF BOWLING	1st Innings					2nd Innings					
Name	O.	M.	R.	W.	Wd. N-b		O.	M.	R.	W.	Wd. N-b
Lillee	35.4	7	102	0	... ...		26.4	8	82	3	... 1
Alderman	30.2	7	79	1	... 5		17	2	42	1	... 8
Lawson	43.1	14	81	7	3 5		19	6	51	1	... 3
Bright	15	7	31	1	... ...		36	18	67	3	... 1

AUSTRALIA

			First Innings		Second Innings	
1	G. M. Wood	W. Australia	c Taylor b Willis	44	not out	62
2	J. Dyson	New South Wales	c Gower b Botham	7	l b w b Dilley	1
3	G. N. Yallop	Victoria	b Dilley	1	c Botham b Willis	3
†4	K. J. Hughes	W. Australia	c Willis b Emburey	42	l b w b Dilley	4
5	T. M. Chappell	New South Wales	c Taylor b Dilley	2	c Taylor b Botham	5
6	A. R. Border	Queensland	c Gatting b Botham	64	not out	12
*7	R. W. Marsh	W. Australia	l b w b Dilley	47		
8	R. J. Bright	Victoria	l b w b Emburey	33		
9	G. F. Lawson	New South Wales	l b w b Willis	5		
10	D. K. Lillee	W. Australia	not out	40		
11	T. M. Alderman	W. Australia	c Taylor b Willis	5		
			B 6, l-b 11, w 6, n-b 32,	55	B , l-b , w 1, n-b 2,	3
			Total	345	Total	90

FALL OF THE WICKETS

1—62 2—62 3—69 4—81 5—167 6—244 7—257 8—268 9—314 10—345
1—2 2—11 3—17 4—62 5— 6— 7— 8— 9— 10—

ANALYSIS OF BOWLING	1st Innings					2nd Innings					
Name	O.	M.	R.	W.	Wd. N-b		O.	M.	R.	W.	Wd. N-b
Willis	27.4	9	50	3	... 24		12	3	35	1	... 2
Dilley	30	8	106	3	4 8		7.5	1	18	2	... ...
Botham	26	8	71	2	2 ...		8	3	10	1	1 ...
Gooch	10	4	28	0	... ...						
Emburey	25	12	35	2	... ...		21	10	24	0	... ...

Umpires—D. O. Oslear & K. E. Palmer   Scorers—E. Solomon & D. K. Sherwood

† Captain   * Wicket-keeper

Australia won the toss and elected to field

could go off and find Alec Bedser and tell him: 'I'm sorry, Alec, but I can't carry on under the present circumstances. It's not fair on me, my family or the team unless you are prepared to offer me a run at the captaincy.'

He told me that the selectors were not prepared to do that whereupon I thanked him for all his help. I immediately went downstairs to tell the waiting cricket writers: 'Before you ask me any questions about the match I have an announcement to make. I have resigned as England's captain.' Immediately I uttered those words I felt a new man. For the first time in a month I felt completely relaxed. I was at peace with the world again.

5 I resign
-and get the sack

I shall always have the utmost respect and admiration for Alec Bedser – big, solid, dependable, absolutely devoted to the game of cricket as he has proved by following up his 236 wickets for England by serving as a selector, the last 13 years as chairman. His reign ended with the selection of the touring party for the 1981–82 tour of India and Sri Lanka. He hands over to Peter May who will be in charge for the 1982 summer but I hope he stays on as one of the three other selectors. 'Big Al', as he is known throughout the cricketing world, is okay; his heart is in the right place.

He has come in for a great deal of stick during his time as chairman. Everybody has their own idea of what the England team should be, and who should be the captain. Some of the letters he has received have been cruel and insulting. But every decision he has taken has been governed by one ideal – to produce the best possible side to make England successful at Test level. Perhaps a more ruthless man might have achieved better results now and again but I doubt it. Even through the unsuccessful times the spirit in the England dressing-room has always been good, everybody pulling for each other. Much of the harmony has been down to the captain. But Alec can also take considerable credit. He has not always agreed one hundred per cent with the final team or tour party chosen. Yet he has accepted the majority verdict with good grace, stoutly defending the player chosen in preference to his own nominee when the public or the press have been critical.

I shall always be grateful to him too. I was one of the youngest players on the 1979–80 tour of Australia but Alec backed me when it was suggested that I should make up the tour selection party along with assistant manager Ken Barrington, skipper Mike

Brearley, vice-captain Bob Willis and himself. The move surprised a number of people. Although I had played in 21 Test matches, I was still regarded as raw material with a reputation for being boisterous, but Alec told various groups throughout the winter: 'That Botham talks a lot of sense, you know, in committee meetings.'

The popular view when I was first appointed England's captain was that I was handed the role more by default than because I showed any signs of being leadership material. Mike Brearley had announced that he would not be available for any future tours, Keith Fletcher had been away from Test cricket for some time, Roger Knight had never played Test cricket and the other county captains were either too old or had been born overseas. Of the players in the England side, they had already tried Geoff Boycott and found him wanting in some way. Bob Willis would have seemed the most natural choice but on his return from Australia, where he had struggled to find his form, there was a doubt about his international future.

Over the years the selectors had been under constant fire for sticking with Mike when many said he wasn't worth his place as a batsman, and by opting for me at least they were going for one player who was reasonably certain of his place – at that time anyway. But I believe there was more to it than that. The things I had said at the selection and planning meetings throughout the Australian tour must have convinced Alec that I could offer more than sheer brute strength and a keen eye.

When my appointment was announced – and criticised – Alec backed me all the way. When doubts about my captaincy ability were raised during the first series against the West Indies at home, he was by my side. When my appointment for the winter tour of the West Indies was attacked in some quarters, he spoke up for me. When they demanded my head at the end of the series, he came to my defence. I shall always be grateful. Yet I feel the selectors let me down in 1981. And Alec himself let me down at Lords.

After I had announced my resignation to the cricketing press, on television and radio after the drawn second Cornhill Test at Lord's, I went to great lengths to stress that there was no animosity, no ill-feeling, and that I had come to the decision simply to protect my family, my team and myself. Later Alec was to speak in a similar vein when he stressed there had been no attempt on my part 'to hold a pistol to the heads of the selectors'.

So far so good. But then, in my opinion, Alec spoiled what had been a perfectly amicable parting of the ways by announcing: 'We were going to sack him anyway.'

I thought that was totally unnecessary. When I saw that their decision to appoint me on a match-by-match basis for the first two Test matches of the series was having a harmful effect on the players around me, I made what I thought was the right move by resigning, leaving them free to appoint somebody else without any feelings of embarrassment. If they were going to make a change, they had got what they wanted without having to announce that it had already been decided I was for the high jump. After what I had been through, I could have done without that final sting.

Only two people knew of my decision when I walked off the field at Lord's on that final evening. Earlier in the day I had talked it over with Bernard Thomas, the England and Warwickshire physiotherapist who is the closest man to the team. He is the man who listens to all our troubles when we are feeling a little low. Early on that final day I had confessed to him that I couldn't carry on if it was going to be on a match-by-match basis. I had also mentioned it to Bob Willis. Officially, England do not have a vice-captain during a series at home but Bob would have been the one to take over if I had been injured or taken ill during a Test match. Both Bernard and Bob were very sympathetic.

Nobody else had the slightest suspicion – at least outside my family. Apart from the announcement that I was going to be sacked anyway, the other unfortunate part of the proceedings was that I did not have an opportunity to tell all the England team personally.

By the time I had seen Alec, spoken to the cricket writers, been interviewed on television and radio, an hour had gone by. When I returned to the England dressing-room less than half the team remained. They were too shocked to say anything and I was grateful for that. It was a very emotional time. I didn't want any inquests. The only thing on my mind was to get away from Lord's and find my wife Kath. Even that was harder than I anticipated.

By the time I had changed and packed, there were reporters, photographers, radio men and television news cameras everywhere. They were looking for me, looking for Kath, and it was some time before we were able to be alone together and I could tell her what had happened. I had not discussed the resignation with her. If I had wanted to stay with the captaincy and the

Geoff Lawson, who rivalled Rodney Hogg as Australia's fastest bowler, had no hesitation in putting in a bouncer now and again against anybody – but he wasn't so hot in dealing with them when he had a bat in his hand. He was forced into a ballet-like pose getting out of the way of this bouncer at Headingley which prompted me to give him another soon after. He turned his back on the second one but left his bat in the way to give Bob Taylor a catch behind the wicket during Australia's first innings of 401 for nine

selectors had backed me for one more match, she would have supported me. But she could also tell how much the whole business had got me down over the five days of the Lord's Test. She suspected that I might quit. And she was very relieved.

I made my decision for three basic reasons. For the sake of my wife. For the sake of the team. For my own peace of mind. In that order.

Kath had spent the most miserable period of her life during my year in charge. It wasn't very pleasant for her when I was in the West Indies and she was back home, constantly reading or listening to criticism of my performances and the team's troubles. Imagine how any wife would feel – whether she was the wife of a

There are many moments during the summer of 1981 that will stay with me. This is one of them. I was forced to duck hurriedly to get out of the way of a second successive beamer from Lawson during my century in England's second innings. I accepted his apology after the first but never forgave him for the second. Fortunately for Lawson, I never had a chance to bowl to him again in the series; Headingley proved to be his last Test of the summer because of a back injury

bank manager, salesman, miner or whatever – if she was constantly told her husband was a failure. It was not a happy situation.

It was to get worse for Kath when I was put on trial before the whole country. She likes to be with me when I am away on Test duty. The Tests provide the few opportunities in the summer when we might have six evenings together in succession. It also helps me to have her around. Yet, during the first Test at Trent Bridge and the second at Lord's she was often forced out of the ground by people I can only bracket together with one word – cowards. Sheer mindless cowards.

Here was a young wife looking after my two young children, Liam and Sarah, and trying to enjoy herself, yet people deliberately sought her out so that they could have a go at me, using the most insulting language. They were not young thoughtless teenagers of the type who are accused of 'hooliganism' on the football terraces and chant obscenities, but 'mature', grown-up men, solid pillars of society who spotted her minding her own business in the crowd or walking around the ground and then launched into a tirade of verbal abuse. They took it out on a defenceless woman, safe and secure in the knowledge that she could not have a go back at them. They were never brave enough to come up to me and tell me what they thought, preferring to shout their abuse from the safety of a crowd. It is not surprising that Kath was driven from the ground on more than one occasion, very close to tears and forced to seek the solitude and comfort of our hotel room or wander around the shops trying to escape.

My match-by-match appointment created abnormal interest in the newspapers, spilling over from the sports pages into the news section. This also made life harder for Kath. From the moment I first took the captaincy she had been in constant demand for interviews etc. Now she was being constantly bothered for her reaction to every little thing that was happening to me. Normally most newspapers have one main cricket writer at a Test match plus a back-up man who scouts around for any odd news item and conducts the after-play interviews. During the summer of 1981 they frequently sent a third reporter – a newsman who was often not sympathetic towards the game, or a female writer seeking the woman's view. Kath was never left in peace.

I'm not saying that being the wife of an England captain is all

I never wear a crash helmet unless I'm facing the world's fastest bowlers on a wicket which suits them. I find them uncomfortable and cumbersome as well as providing an additional means of getting out. By this I mean there is always a danger of them dropping on your wicket when they fall off. Geoff Boycott's did just that when he was forced to jerk his head out of the way of a Dennis Lillee bouncer at Headingley

misery. The appointment opened many doors for us, took us to places and events to which we would never have gone or been invited. It has given both of us privileges few people can enjoy. Under normal circumstances it can be an enjoyable life. The circumstances at the start of the 1981 season made things far from normal. Kath suffered far more than I did. I couldn't carry on, for her sake.

Then there was the welfare of the side to consider. Captains in England have been appointed for just one Test at the start of the series on three or four occasions before. It is perhaps not a satisfactory situation. It doesn't help the captain in charge. It doesn't particularly help the team. They function much better in a settled atmosphere, a smooth-running dressing-room. But once doesn't do too much harm; when it happened twice I noticed a change in the atmosphere.

There was no lack of effort. There was no lack of co-operation. But I began to sense at Lord's that the players were unsettled, simply because they had no idea what the future had in store. No captain can get the best out of the men serving him if his instructions are being questioned. By the very nature of my match-by-match trial, the whole country was being asked to sit in judgment on my every move. At Lord's it got to the stage where I felt that if I took my handkerchief out of my pocket and blew my nose the Test Match Special experts on radio would be sitting around discussing what particular signal this was, the television experts analysing it. The other ten players with me would have been strange human beings indeed if they had not started to question – if only to themselves – my every move.

I know Alec Bedser argued that the selectors were only doing what the Australians had been doing for years in their home series. They never appoint a captain for the whole series. But, as I said earlier, why should England suddenly start to copy what the Australians do? In fact, it doesn't quite work on a match-by-match basis in Australia either. They may not appoint a captain for the series but it has not been often that they have switched horses in the middle. The captain appointed for the first Test is usually sure he is going to get the rest, barring a sudden and drastic loss of form.

Then there was the additional pressure on myself: I have to admit it got to me at Lord's. The captaincy itself never bothered me, never imposed a strain I could not handle despite my lack of personal success. I wrote earlier that I felt it was all coming back, the crisis was over. The pressure which finally told at Lord's was caused simply by the uncertainty – the feeling of not knowing what was going to happen next, or where I was heading. I couldn't plan a campaign. My hands were tied.

I hated that last day at Lord's. It is one day above all others I shall want to forget as quickly as possible. From my seat on the England dressing-room balcony on the right-hand side of the pavilion I could look across and see Alec Bedser, Charlie Elliott, Brian Close and John Edrich huddled together on the balcony of the players' dining-room for most of the morning. I knew I was the subject of their discussion. It was an eerie feeling.

Close friends have since told me that I became a changed man over the days immediately before Lord's and during the Test match. I wasn't particularly aware of it but they have said that I went around in a little world of my own. I would start a conversation and then drift away, my mind wandering so that I was seldom taking any notice of what people were saying to me. When friends dropped in they soon noticed I contributed little to the discussions, which is very unlike me. Instead I sat and stared – at anything. Out of the window, up at the ceiling, perhaps at the television set but taking nothing in.

There was also one other important consideration – my county, Somerset. Joel Garner and Viv Richards were back with us after missing the previous summer because of the West Indies tour, so we had a great opportunity of picking up one, possibly two if not three, of the domestic honours available. In fact I fancied us for all four titles, being the super-optimist that I am, and even struck a bet in the West Indies that we would make cricketing history. But the mood I was in at Lord's was never going to help Somerset's cause.

The first of our objectives that summer was the Benson and Hedges Cup and the day after the Lord's Test match we had a crucial semi-final to play against Kent at Taunton. I needed to feel right for that game. And the only way of getting right was to settle the captaincy issue once and for all. If I wasn't going to be named for more than the third Test at Headingley, I would have to call it a day.

Whether I made up my mind to resign – victory at Lord's would not have altered my decision – before the selectors decided to sack me, I don't know. From what I have since been told about the

---

Boycott was not the only one to lose his helmet at Headingley. Kim Hughes, Australia's captain, also lost his when he took evasive action against a short pitched delivery from Bob Willis.

timing of events, I think I was first. I have since learned, too, that the decision was not unanimous. I understand that one selector was all in favour of giving me the captaincy for Headingley, another was adamant that I should go. The latter had his way. That was me finished.

At least three good points emerged from my resignation/sacking. Firstly, it was pleasing to hear that Alec Bedser made no criticism of my actual leadership ability when he said the selectors had opted for a change. He went as far as to say that there was no reason why I should not be back in charge after a time. 'We were a bit worried as to Ian's form. We felt that he is improving as a captain but over these last few months he's had a rough time. The West Indies was a really hard tour and he has come back, but his form hasn't been too good. I think his family have been harassed, he has been harassed and we think it would be best to give him a rest from the captaincy and give him a chance to get back into the groove again,' explained Alec.

Almost the first question I was asked by everybody when it was known I was going concerned my preference as to my successor. I had no hesitation in saying Mike Brearley. It was a selfish choice because he is by far and away the best captain I have served. If I was to stay in the side – and England have had a habit of ignoring sacked captains for a while to avoid any embarrassment – with a chance of finding my true form, Mike was the ideal man to help me.

The final good point was that the pressure I had been under dissolved instantly I had spoken to Alec Bedser. I felt as free as a bird as I drove to Taunton that Tuesday evening for the next day's Benson and Hedges Cup semi-final. I was just in the right mood to share the new ball the next morning with Joel Garner and pluck out the wickets of Bob Woolmer and Mark Benson in my opening spell to put the skids under Kent at nine for two and help secure Somerset's place in the final – back at Lord's.

6 Back among the runs and wickets -third Test

'You don't fancy hanging around on this wicket for a day and a half, do you?' I said to Graham Dilley when he walked to the wicket to join me at Headingley. 'No way,' he replied. 'Right,' I said. 'Come on, let's give it some humpty.'

And with those simple words the greatest comeback in Test history was born on Monday 20 July 1981, resulting in our incredible 18 run victory the following day after we had been forced to follow on. Only once before in the history of Test matches between the two countries had such a feat been performed. (That was in Sydney in 1894–95 when England fought back to win by 10 runs.)

The amazing events at Headingley over the final one and a half days apparently brought the country almost to a standstill. It was reported that share dealing on the Stock Exchange ground to a halt when Bob Willis went through the Australian second innings like a raging bull clearing the streets in Pamplona, Spain. In high streets everywhere little groups gathered on pavements to watch the action through the windows of television rental shops. Housewives who had not the slightest interest in cricket, put down their housework to switch on. Business meetings were adjourned for a while – and those that couldn't be adjourned were constantly interrupted as news of each fallen wicket was announced.

On the field itself I was leaping around like a two-year-old – exactly a fortnight after I had walked off the field at Lord's feeling more like a 200-year-old, determined to rid myself of the England captaincy and wondering whether I was going to talk my way out of the Test side at the same time.

It would not have surprised me if I had been dropped. If Mike Brearley had not been appointed in my place I might well have been. Going on my Test form alone I probably did not deserve a place, although my allround potential helped the balance of the side. If any other captain had been brought in from outside the Test squad it would have been understandable if he had not wanted me around for a while to avoid any possible embarrassment.

I wanted to stay in the side. I wanted to help in any way I could to beat the Australians and make sure the Ashes stayed in England. I'm not an Australian admirer, having lived there for three winters playing cricket. I find the country big and empty. Mike encouraged me to think there was still a place for me when

During the summer of 1981 we all thought it was worth letting John Dyson have a few deliveries to hook at. He usually goes for the stroke which must give the bowler a chance of getting his wicket. I gave him one during his first Test century at Headingley but he played this one perfectly to chalk up one of his fourteen boundaries

he talked about his return to Test cricket the day after he had been reappointed captain.

He said that as he saw it one of his main tasks was to nurse me back to full Test health with the bat and ball. He was given the chance to do it because he was offered a three-match appointment, despite the fact that he was not available to lead England in India on the winter tour. The selectors had obviously brought him back with one objective in mind – winning the Ashes. They left their options open for India by leaving themselves free to pick another captain for the final Test at the Oval.

For the first three days of the Headingley Test match it didn't

Another bouncer from me to Dyson but the Australian opener again met this one perfectly on his way to his 102 in Australia's 401 for nine declared. Yet the stroke was to prove his undoing in the second innings when he hooked at Bob Willis only to give a catch behind. It was part of Australia's remarkable collapse which was to give us our 18 run victory

No, I hadn't dozed off during my century at Headingley even if the cameraman does appear to have caught me with my eyes closed. This is during England's second innings as I connect with a sweep stroke which was to bring me yet another boundary

look as though Mike was going to be any more successful than I had been. By that stage Australia had scored 401 for nine declared, we had been bowled out for 174 and were six for one in our second innings.

By the Saturday evening Kim Hughes was already claiming the Ashes in the belief that he was on the verge of going two ahead in the series with three matches to play. He was to discover there is nothing so dangerous as an England side that has been written off. This one had not only been written off but was frequently described as 'pathetic' over the first three days at Leeds. The gibes hurt. Some of the attacks became too personal for our liking. But it all helped to rekindle the fire and make us come out fighting.

We didn't fight too well during those first three days on another wicket which was not exactly the type on which you expect to play Test cricket. The ball is always likely to move about when there is cloud around at Headingley, more than on any other Test ground in the country. We all accept that. What we did not expect was the irregular bounce just as we had found at Trent Bridge. It wasn't to help us when Kim Hughes won the toss and chose to bat first, no doubt remembering the scare he had received at Lord's. He didn't want to risk batting last this time.

Mike's reappointment had forced one change in the side. A batsman had to go to accommodate him and Bob Woolmer was the one to miss out. There was one other change in the bowling of a 'horses for courses' type with Chris Old, who had taken over the Yorkshire captaincy, brought back in place of Mike Hendrick to bowl in conditions he knows so well.

I can reveal that we almost went into the match without Bob Willis who later provided the final link in our dramatic victory with his eight wickets on the last day. I understand that the team was picked without Willis who had been ordered to rest completely for a week following his chest infection during the second Test at Lord's. The fast bowling attack was to be made up of Dilley, Old, Hendrick and myself. Then, only a matter of hours before the team was due to be released, Mike had a change of mind, the selectors had a ring around on the telephone and Willis was retained with Hendrick dropping out. Did somebody mention somewhere you also need a little luck to be a successful captain?

Not that luck was our companion on that first day when the Australians repeatedly played and missed as the ball moved off the wicket, swung through the air and bounced alarmingly on occasions. Old bowled well enough to have taken five wickets before lunch. Instead he went wicketless as the Australians survived a day-long flirtation with disaster to make 203 for three with opener John Dyson producing the first century of the series.

There was never a suggestion of a collapse. Wood and Dyson put on 55 for the first wicket before Wood was beaten by an inswinger from me and caught leg-before. Dyson and Chappell then added 94 in 45 overs before Chappell attempted to cut Willey and edged a catch behind. Finally Dyson and Hughes took the score to 196, at which stage Dyson was bowled by Dilley just

after completing his century in 294 minutes with 14 fours. Once
again we were up against it. We left the field wondering just how
the Australians had escaped on a wicket we should have been able
to exploit to full advantage. Perhaps, with the exception of Old,
we didn't bowl well enough, became a little carried away with the
bounce when we might have done better in pitching the ball up
relying on seam and swing. Whatever the reason, we needed to
strike early the next day.

We didn't manage to do that but the day brought my first
five-wicket haul in a Test match for more than a year – and thus
produced the evidence my critics wanted to support their conten-
tion that the captaincy had affected my ability. I think I would
have taken those wickets anyway, five of the six that were to fall
on that Friday.

Throughout most of the first day and again at the start of the
second, Mike had bowled me in fairly short spells. Usually they
were four overs long, once I think he tried me for just three overs.
We were not really getting anywhere and I was certainly not
working up any kind of rhythm. In the end, just as Hughes and
Yallop were threatening us with a century partnership and had
taken the Australian total beyond 300, I said to Mike: 'Give me
the ball, keep me on for a long spell and I'll get the wickets for
you.'

Mike did exactly that and I was true to my word. The next five
wickets were all mine, starting with Hughes when he was just
eleven runs short of his century. He mistimed an attempted drive
against me and offered a simple return catch. Border was the next
to go when I had him leg-before, then Yallop who got an inside
edge attempting to cut me.

Lawson became my fifth victim when I dropped one short. He
turned his back on it but conveniently left his bat hanging out in
mid-air for the ball to lob off the shoulder and give Taylor a
simple catch. When I yorked Marsh soon after, Hughes called it a
day shortly before the close so that he could have a couple of
overs at us. After tea on that second day I bowled 16.5 overs
without a break, taking five for 35 as the Australians slipped from
332 for four to 401 for nine. I like bowling in longish spells and
would have given myself one some time before Mike listened to
my pleadings.

I was headline news again the next morning. That evening the newspaper 'quote' men were asking to see me once more. But there was a difference. This time I had brought the pressure on myself and it was the type of pressure I could live with.

If further evidence was required that my Test career had been saved by the switch in captaincy, I furnished it on the third day when I scored my first half-century in the last 20 Test innings I had played for England to help save us from complete humiliation. Against the attack of Lillee, Alderman and Lawson – cleverly used by Hughes and making full use of the conditions as we should have done – our batting folded disastrously. We were bowled out for 174 and then sent in again 227 runs behind when Australia enforced the follow-on.

My half-century was double the next highest score, that of 24 by Gower. I took over when Gatting was out with the score at 87 and stayed to score exactly 50 of the 79 runs added whilst I was at the crease before I was caught behind off my gloves. The end of the innings was not far away and worse was to follow when we batted again and lost Goochie. He had the unhappy experience of facing just four balls on that Saturday – one in the morning and three in the evening – and being out twice.

The celebrations were the exclusive right of the Australians that evening. Hughes was celebrating what he believed was the recapture of the Ashes, Lillee his thirty-second birthday and Marsh becoming a new recordholder in Test cricket. The catch he had taken off me had brought his number of Test victims to 264, one more than the previous record set by Alan Knott. He had taken them in 22 fewer Tests, a large percentage of them falling to him through the bowling of his Western Australian team-mate Dennis Lillee. They had been drafted into the Test side together against Ray Illingworth's England side in Australia in 1970–71.

I gather their celebrations went on long into the night. At that stage we had nothing to cheer about, although I did my best to ease our tension with a barbecue at my home. It was a rather subdued event at first but, by the end of the evening, we had shaken off our disappointment and vowed to show the Australians what English Test cricket was all about.

We just didn't expect it to happen so soon. With only nine wickets left and still 222 runs needed to make Australia bat again,

I think most of us had given up the third Test for dead. I certainly had. I checked out of the England team hotel on the Monday morning expecting the match to finish that day. I was not alone. We pack and unpack so often, it is a chore. I didn't mind unpacking again that Monday evening – especially with a century under my belt.

Our only real hope of escaping from the match on that Monday morning was if the weather came to our aid. The forecast was for unsettled weather. It had rained heavily at times on the Sunday rest day and might still save us. That also required us to bat well in between the showers on a wicket which was certain to produce a lethal, unplayable delivery every now and again. Those deliveries duly arrived.

We started the day at six for one. By lunch we were 78 for four which represented something of a recovery with Boycott resisting stubbornly, Willey fighting as if his life depended on him staying at the crease. We had been 41 for four at one stage with Brearley and Gower both caught in the slips and Gatting out leg-before. With no sign of the rain and Willey top-edging a catch to short third man with still another 122 runs needed to make Australia bat again, the decision to book out of the hotel that morning appeared thoroughly justified when I walked out to the crease. Our score was then 105 for five, soon to become 133 for six when Boycott's 215 minute vigil was ended by Alderman. Then it was 135 for seven as Taylor offered a simple catch to short-leg off the same bowler.

Above: I have always rated Graham Dilley's ability with the bat as well as the ball. Tall, powerfully built with a keen eye, he strikes the ball well as he shows here when driving Terry Alderman to the boundary during our 117 run eighth-wicket partnership in 80 minutes at Headingley

Below: Pitch anything up to Graham Dilley and it is asking for punishment. Drop the ball a little short and he is not so effective. He was only inches away from giving a catch when he attempted to hook during his first Test half-century at Headingley

That was the moment when Dilley strode out and we decided together that 'a bit of humpty' was the only solution. It lit the touch paper that was to set cricket alight again in England, and blow a fuse in Australia.

I had already courted disaster once or twice by then, taking gigantic swings without connecting against Lillee and Alderman in an attempt to take the fight to the Australians. It must have alarmed many people watching. It certainly alarmed umpire Barrie Meyer.

With the tail to come I couldn't see any point in trying to play safe. Dilley is a good, clean and powerful striker of the ball. So is Old when he is in the mood. I reasoned that the only way we stood a chance was by turning the tables and attempting to dominate the Australian fast bowlers who had spent two days dominating us. I couldn't see how we were going to get anywhere pushing forward defensively down the line against bowlers who were still making the ball move off the wicket and bounce. That is a deadly combination.

Some of my early scoring strokes were a bit risky, not going quite where I intended in squirting them between the slips, occasionally over the arc of close catchers Hughes had set. There again, I reasoned that if I gave it the big wind-up the edges would fly so thick and furiously it was going to need a brilliant piece of fielding to hold on to the chance. My reasoning proved correct soon after Dilley joined me when an attempted cover drive against Alderman ended up going through the gully area where Bright was standing. Technically, I suppose, it was a risk because Bright actually got one hand to the ball. But the ball went at him so quickly it was more of an instinctive reaction in thrusting out his left hand than a serious attempt at taking a catch. I would have considered myself extremely unlucky if the ball had stuck.

A moment to treasure. I take time out in the third Test to relax for a second after scoring my century during England's second innings. It was my first match after returning to the ranks following my spell as captain and all the pressures of being 'on trial' had vanished

Dilley was absolutely magnificent. Within half an hour the Australian pace attack was starting to wilt. I was helped by the fact that Dilley is a left-hander when it comes to batting which meant that the Australian bowlers were constantly being forced to change their line. They, like us on the first day, bowled too short hoping the bounce would get us into trouble. And, suddenly, they started to tire.

Mike had been heavily criticised after the first day for not playing John Emburey's off-spin on a dry, bare wicket. He had gone for four pace bowlers instead and judged the wicket well. Australia had gone for only three, supported by Bright. They paid for their mistake on that Monday afternoon when they could have done with a fourth pace bowler to help relieve Lillee, Alderman and Lawson. Not that Dilley or myself were objecting.

I had been at the wicket for 45 minutes by the time Dilley joined me yet he was to match me almost stroke for stroke during our 117 run eighth wicket partnership in 80 minutes. He actually outscored me during our first 30 minutes together, scoring 25 runs to my 16. By the time he was bowled by Alderman for a Test highest score of 56, I had actually scored 57 towards the stand in taking my total to 80. England's innings was starting to live again.

Some of Dilley's strokes, just like mine, did not go exactly where he intended, but he also employed a full wind-up and attacked with all his strength, even though he did not have the advantage of being able to use one of Goochie's bats as I did.

Above: This was one event I didn't win during the 1981 summer. I wanted to be first to the boundary after my unbeaten 149 during England's second innings at Headingley but the well-wishers came swarming on to the outfield to catch me before I reached the safety of the dressing-room

Below: It was not until some time after my century at Headingley that I was able to savour it fully. I found a quiet corner of the dressing-room where I could puff on my favourite cigars and reflect on the day's events. At the time I didn't know they were to lead to our staggering comeback and one of the most famous victories in the history of Test cricket

Goochie likes the heaviest bat around and I pinched one of his for my innings. He hadn't used it much during the match and I thought there were a few runs left in it. By the time I lost Dilley as a partner we had at least made sure that Australia would not beat us by an innings. But we were only 25 runs ahead and I thought we needed another 125 before we could think seriously of bowling Australia out. We had just two wickets left.

Chris Old, another left-handed batsman who has the ability to score many more runs than he has done, took over where Dilley left off. Really it is a tragedy that Old is regarded as a tail-ender in the England side when he has scored six first-class centuries. He should be batting just after me with his ability. He produced that ability when we needed it most in helping me to put on 67 for the ninth wicket and take us to 319 before he was beaten by a Lawson yorker. He was at the crease when I edged Lawson through the slip area for four to reach my seventh Test century. It was not the best of strokes but I couldn't have cared less at that moment.

Mike led all the other players out on to the balcony to join in the applause. He made his usual signal in such circumstances, telling me to make sure I stayed out there, and I gave him my usual signal back, the type Harvey Smith has been known to use. It's a little sideshow we have indulged in before. I was to learn later that of those 103 runs I had scored 82 in boundaries with 19 fours and a six which flowed from one of my best strokes when driving Alderman straight back over his head. I enjoyed that one.

There were still 45 minutes of the day remaining when Willis, our last man, came out to join me. He's not the best of batters, possessing one main stroke, a forward lunge which seems to take him halfway down the wicket. But he knows how to survive, as he did a year earlier when staying almost three hours and helping Willey to his first Test century against the West Indies at The Oval. The pair added 117 for the final wicket to earn a draw. Even so I had some doubts about him being able to stay around when it was essential that we crashed on as heavily as possible.

The new ball was going to be available first thing on the last morning, by which time Lillee and Co would have benefited from a night's rest. We had to take every run that was going, which meant me trying to engineer most of the strike. It worked well until the final delivery of the day when I wanted a single to make sure I would be able to take the first over – and the new ball – in the morning. It was a risky run, needing a direct hit to produce a wicket. We both set off together but Willis hesitated halfway up the wicket which almost proved fatal. It was my fault entirely. I went for the run shouting 'go, go, go'. In all the tremendous noise from the crowd, the shouting of the Australians hoping for a run-out, Willis thought I was saying 'no, no, no'. He began to think of turning back when I passed him going like the wind in the opposite direction. He got into full stride again and made it safely to the crease.

In the last two hours after tea we had scored 175 runs off 27 overs but we were still only 124 ahead at 351 for nine. Not enough, I thought, as I walked off, not knowing that I had become the first English player to take five or more wickets in an innings and score a century in the same match in an Ashes game. The best was still to come.

We had to settle for a 129 run lead when we returned for that last dramatic, pulsating day. There was just time for me to add one more boundary, making it 27 fours in all plus a six, before Willis edged Alderman to second slip. I was one short of 150 but had still managed my highest Test score. It left Australia needing 130 to win, not enough to extend them. And yet we felt it was the type of wicket that if one batsman fell we had a chance of getting another wicket straightaway. We couldn't allow one man to dig himself in, but Dyson threatened to do just that when we launched our final fling. We couldn't afford to give easy runs away either, but Dilley did just that with eleven coming off his first two overs.

Mike had opened with me in the hope that I might be able to swing the ball when it was new, and brought Dilley on because he often managed to strike very quickly. The move didn't work this time, at least as far as Dilley was concerned.

I did manage a quick wicket. In my second over Wood attempted an off-drive against me but the ball moved enough to find the edge of the bat and Taylor completed a simple catch behind. Australia were 13 for one with their innings nine minutes old. But then nothing happened for over an hour with Willis bowling from the football stand end at Headingley while I gave way to Old.

Nothing happened, from our point of view that is. Everything was going smoothly as far as the Australians were concerned, with the score moving to 56 which meant they needed only 74 to win. Then it all happened for us as well when Willis switched to the other end. He said later: 'I told Mike I was getting too old to bowl into the wind and uphill so I'd better have the wind to help me.'

The result of the switch was dramatic. During the previous two Tests and again in the first innings at Headingley Willis had been concerned about his run-up and the number of no balls he was giving away through over-stepping. He had suffered similarly against the West Indies and it worried him so much that he virtually talked himself out of the Test side. This time Mike told him to forget it. 'Just run up and let the ball go as fast as you can. I'll do the worrying about the no balls,' Mike told him. Willis did just that. With his extra few inches, he discovered bounce no other bowler had produced during the match.

Eyes fixed in a glare which must have been frightening in itself to any batsman, Willis then ran in to strangle the Australian innings with the finest bowling performance of his career, the best by an England bowler in a Test match at Headingley. It was a tribute to his strength and determination. And to the skill of the surgeon who had stitched his dodgy knees and enabled him to carry on playing to produce a spell of such devastation. It was only a couple of months after Willis had said goodbye to us in the West Indies and flown home wondering whether he would ever play again.

Chappell was the first to feel the effect of Willis' change of ends producing a shortish ball which rose steeply to find the shoulder of the bat as Chappell did his best to fend it off but edged a catch behind. Even Greg Chappell would have struggled with that delivery. Trevor Chappell was not good enough. And that was just the spur we needed. Australia were 56 for two and soon 58 for four in the last dramatic over before lunch, which must have made the meal pretty well indigestible.

Hughes was the first to go in that over, beaten by pace and edging a catch which forced me to dive to hold. Three balls later Yallop was following Hughes back, doing his best to get on top of another shortish delivery which Gatting did well to hold at short-leg. In eleven deliveries Willis had taken three wickets without conceding a run to throw the Australian innings into confusion.

But Dyson was still batting steadily. We desperately needed his wicket and that of their remaining hope, the solidly defiant Border. They were halfway to their target of 130 when Border fell. Old had been brought back at the football stand end and bowled Border with one that cut back quite sharply off the wicket. Three ducks sitting pretty right in the middle of the Australian innings. Hughes, Yallop and Border all in a row.

That still left Dyson. But not for long as Willis swept in to clean up the rest, finding hidden reserves of energy we thought he no longer possessed. Every time those long and delicate legs of his seemed about to buckle under the strain of giving everything he had, he came up with a wicket to send fresh life surging through his body. He raced in to let Dyson have a shortish delivery which the batsman should have ignored. Instead he went for the hook, got the thinnest of top edges and Taylor did the rest. Now we were in sight of victory with Australia 68 for six.

But we spent many agonising moments before we were able to scrape home. One of the worst came when Marsh hooked at a shortish ball from Willis. My first thought was that the ball was going for six over long leg. Then the ball started to drop as Dilley stationed himself beneath it. It was an awkward, swirling ball just in from the boundary edge. Dilley couldn't afford to take his eyes off it for one second but at the same time he was worried about putting a foot over the boundary line. There was a great sigh all round on the field when he not only held the catch but stayed inside the line. A couple more blows like that from Marsh and it would have been all over.

The next man, Lawson, was no trouble but Taylor was grateful for the catch which took him past John Murray's record of 1,270 first-class catches. That was Australia 75 for eight with 55 runs wanted. Then came the big worry.

Lillee joined Bright and together they restored Australia's hopes as Mike was left doing a juggling act with his field. Most fielders were in a close catching position when these two teamed up. Gradually Mike was forced to put first one man back to protect the boundary and then another as they threatened our grip on the game. They had reduced the target to 38 and galloped towards victory when Bright took 10 from one over against Old, and Lillee weighed in with six in the next over from Willis.

Suddenly the close-in field was reduced to three slips and a gully as Gatting was withdrawn from the short-leg position and put at mid-on. And he produced the next heart-stopping moment. Lillee fancied his chances of hitting a four over the top of Gatting's head against Willis but misjudged his drive. For one moment we thought Gatting had misjudged the ball too. He started to go backwards, stopped, started coming in again and finally dived full length in front of him to take the chance an inch or so above the ground. Lillee out for 17, Australia 110 for nine, 20 still wanted with last man Alderman entering.

And still there were shocks to come. After Old's one wayward over I took over at the football end and Old took my place in the slips. Off my second ball Alderman edged straight to Old but he dropped it. Against my fifth ball Alderman got another edge, this time the ball flying off much faster to Old's left. He got a hand to it but couldn't hold it. Technically it was another chance. In reality he did well to get a hand to it but that didn't help him feel any better. Nor the rest of us.

As it happened it didn't matter. In the next over from Willis that was all history and we had won by 18 runs to level the series. Won with the best sight ever seen on a cricket field as Bright's middle stump was sent hurtling out of the ground when he missed an attempted drive. Willis had achieved the impossible. Not only Headingley but the whole country went berserk it seemed. The

---

Above: There is never a dull moment when Dennis Lillee is bowling. There is never any doubt either when he believes he has taken a wicket, part of the attraction of this great fast bowler. He already has his hand up claiming another wicket after inducing a disappointed David Gower into giving a catch to gully during the first Test at Trent Bridge

Below: Not satisfied with one finger upraised, Dennis Lillee points two to the heavens in celebration of having Graham Gooch out leg-before in the fifth Test match at Old Trafford. Graham was to lose his Test place after this match, never coming to terms with the Australian attack after his heroic efforts against the West Indies during the previous twelve months

Above: Although I always enjoy watching Dennis Lillee in action, the outcome is not pleasant every time. There was nothing to smile about for me on this occasion as he wins another appeal during his five-wicket performance in our second innings of the first Test at Trent Bridge. It helped bring about our defeat in the first match of the Ashes series

Opposite: Dennis Lillee doesn't win them all either. He shows his disappointment clearly when he failed to find the edge of my bat during my century at Headingley. He is no longer the fast bowler he was, losing that edge in pace he once possessed. But he is still one of the most effective bowlers in the world with his ability to cut the ball either way off the seam

England v. Australia

Third Test Match

Thursday, Friday, Saturday, Monday & Tuesday, 16th, 17th, 18th, 20th & 21st July 1981

ENGLAND WON BY 18 RUNS

ENGLAND

First Innings			Second Innings	
1—G. Boycott, b Lawson	12		lbw Alderman	46
2—G. A. Gooch, lbw Alderman	2		c Alderman b Lillee	0
*3—J. M. Brearley, c Marsh b Alderman	10		c Alderman b Lillee	14
4—D. I. Gower, c Marsh b Lawson	24		c Border b Alderman	9
5—M. W. Gatting, lbw Lillee	15		lbw Alderman	1
6—P. Willey, b Lawson	8		c Dyson b Lillee	33
7—I. T. Botham, c Marsh b Lillee	50		not out	149
†8—R. W. Taylor, c Marsh b Lillee	5		c Bright b Alderman	1
9—R. G. D. Willis, not out	1		c Border b Alderman	2
10—G. R. Dilley, c and b Lillee	13		b Alderman	56
11—C. M. Old, c Border b Alderman	0		b Lawson	29
Extras	34		Extras	16
Total	174		Total	356

FALL OF WICKETS—

First Innings: 1-12 2-40 3-42 4-84 5-87 6-112 7-148 8-166 9-167

Second Innings: 1-0 2-18 3-37 4-41 5-105 6-133 7-135 8-252 9-319

Bowlers	Overs	Mdns.	Runs	Wkts.
Lillee	18·5	7	49	4
Alderman	19	4	59	3
Lawson	13	3	32	3

Bowlers	Overs	Mdns.	Runs	Wkts.
Lillee	25	6	94	3
Alderman	35·3	6	135	6
Lawson	23	4	96	1
Bright	4	0	15	0

* Denotes Captain   † Denotes Wicket Keeper

Umpires: B. J. Meyer and D. L. Evans
Scorers: E. I. Lester and D. Sherwood

AUSTRALIA

First Innings			Second Innings	
1—J. Dyson, b Dilley	102		c Taylor b Willis	34
2—G. M. Wood, lbw Botham	34		c Taylor b Botham	10
3—T. M. Chappell, c Taylor b Willey	27		c Taylor b Willis	8
*4—K. J. Hughes, c and b Botham	89		c Botham b Willis	0
5—G. N. Yallop, c Taylor b Botham	58		c Gatting b Willis	0
6—A. R. Border, lbw Botham	8		b Old	0
†7—R. W. Marsh, b Botham	28		c Dilley b Willis	4
8—R. J. Bright, b Dilley	7		b Willis	19
9—D. K. Lillee, not out	3		c Gatting b Willis	17
10—G. F. Lawson, c Taylor b Botham	13		c Taylor b Willis	1
11—T. M. Alderman, not out	0		not out	0
Extras	32		Extras	18
Total (for 9 wickets declared)	401		Total	111

FALL OF WICKETS—

First Innings: 1-55 2-149 3-196 4-220 5-332 6-354 7-357 8-396 9-401

Second Innings: 1-13 2-56 3-58 4-58 5-65 6-68 7-74 8-75 9-110

Bowlers	Overs	Mdns.	Runs	Wkts.
Willis	30	8	72	0
Old	43	14	91	0
Dilley	27	4	78	2
Botham	39·2	11	95	6
Willey	13	2	31	1
Boycott	3	2	2	0

Bowlers	Overs	Mdns.	Runs	Wkts.
Botham	7	3	14	1
Dilley	2	0	11	0
Willis	15·1	3	43	8
Old	9	1	21	1
Willey	3	1	4	0

Hours of Play: Thursday to Monday, 11.00 a.m. to 6.00 p.m.
Tuesday, 10.30 a.m. to 5.00 p.m. or 5.30 p.m.

Lunch: 1.00 p.m. to 1.40 p.m. (Tuesday 12.30 p.m. to 1.10 p.m.)

Tea: 3.40 to 4.00 p.m.
(Tuesday 3.10 p.m. to 3.30 p.m.)

rush to salute the country's new sporting heroes was on. And I was back home.

There was bedlam in the England dressing-room for the next two hours. Photographers, newspaper men, television crews and microphones were everywhere. Wellwishers were continually banging on the door as we drank our victory champagne. While on the outfield in front of the pavilion hundreds of supporters cheered, cheered and cheered again. I felt particularly happy for Peter Willey. This was his nineteenth Test match for England, having made his debut on the same Headingley ground against the West Indies back in 1976. Yet this was the first time he had sipped champagne denoting an England victory. How he enjoyed it. 'This tastes different somehow,' he said. 'All the other victory champagne I've drunk has made me feel sick.'

It was all too much to take in. Bob Willis looked no more cheerful in the dressing-room than he had bowling against the Australians out in the middle. He confessed later that the enormity of his feat did not sink in until he was driving home and many miles away from Headingley. It took him that long to wind down.

There was no time for me to savour the victory as I would like to have done or to celebrate my return to form. That evening I had a date 130 miles or so down the motorway with my Somerset colleagues. We were playing Northants the next day in the first round of the new Nat West Bank Trophy. I was hoping it would be a double celebration on the Wednesday evening – England back in the Ashes hunt, Somerset through to the quarter-finals. Instead we were well beaten and my hopes of four trophies for my county as well as the Ashes were dashed.

7 Why I did not want to bowl - fourth Test

Much has been made of the fact that I hadn't wanted to bowl immediately before I took five wickets for one run and sent Australia crashing to their second staggering successive defeat in the fourth Test at Edgbaston. It completed an England comeback that was almost as miraculous as the one at Headingley less than a fortnight earlier. But it has been used mainly as another piece of evidence to suggest that I was not capable of captaining a side and looking after myself properly as a player when it came to playing for my country. The implication was that I would not have put myself on if I had still been in control and England would have lost the chance of going 2–1 ahead in the Ashes series – always assuming we would have won at Leeds under my leadership.

I told Mike I didn't think I was the one to bring on when he asked me to have another go and suggested he should try Peter Willey instead. I think I was right at the time. I still think I was right.

By the time I did come on to bowl the over the Australian situation had changed dramatically. They had lost the wicket of Allan Border to an explosive delivery from John Emburey just when it seemed the stocky left-hander was winning the match in their quest to score 151. Suddenly it had become a completely different ball game.

The wicket had had nothing really to offer me when Mike suggested I should take over from Bob Willis with Border and Kent having added 18 in their fifth wicket partnership. They were both playing Willis quite comfortably at the time. Emburey's off-spin was their main concern. That is why I suggested Willey should be given a turn for the first time in the match. The pitch was helping the odd ball to turn. Willey is a different type of off-spinner to Emburey and he might present them with a problem they had not come across before in their innings. It was certainly worth a try. Mike agreed.

There was one more over from Emburey to get through first. He bowled a delivery which leapt up at Border giving him no opportunity to control it as Mike Gatting took the catch at short-leg. It meant that one end was now open and I needed no second invitation to jump in then, wave Willey away after he had gone through his warm-up exercises and begin those last fateful 28 deliveries.

But all that happened long after we had been labelled 'pathetic' once more when bowled out in our first innings for 189 on a wicket which, although not quite as placid as the usual Edgbaston surfaces, deserved to produce more runs. Not only were *we* labelled 'pathetic' but that charge was also levelled against the Australians when we managed to keep their expected first innings lead down to 69 runs.

England had kept the same victorious 12 on duty as at Heading-ley, although one change was forced on us before the match, another was made in the actual side to suit the conditions, and we made a switch in batting order.

Just after the team had been selected Dilley damaged his right shoulder playing for Kent. He was ordered to rest and it was thought that he would recover in time for the Test. Unfortunately for him, it stiffened up drastically on the drive up to the Midlands on the Wednesday for the practice session and he couldn't raise his right arm more than shoulder high. Mike Hendrick was sent for as cover but was left out of the final team to accommodate Emburey's off-spin. The change in the batting order was made to allow Goochie to drop down into the middle order to see if a spell away from the new ball might help him recover the devastating touch he had produced against the West Indies. Mike Brearley took over his opening role.

The Australians made two changes in their side. They dropped Chappell to make way for the elegance of Martin Kent, who had shown improved form against the county sides, and Rodney Hogg returned as fast bowler in place of Lawson who pulled out with a back strain which proved severe enough to keep him out of the rest of the tour.

That was a great pity as far as I was concerned. I had been

looking forward to meeting up with Lawson again after two
deliveries he had bowled at me during my century at Headingley.
They were beamers, deliveries which come through around head
height without bouncing. They were bowled in succession too.
One can be quite accidental with a ball slipping out of a sweaty
hand, I've bowled some myself now and again. But two in succession? That's stretching it a bit too far. As I ducked frantically out
of the way of the second I couldn't help wondering whether they
had anything to do with the fact that I had bounced him in
Australia's first innings. Yes, I was looking forward to meeting
Lawson again!

The change in batting order worked for Mike, when he won the
toss and batted first, to the extent that he made 48 runs which was
22 runs more than I made – and mine was our next highest score.
Mike's contribution on that first day may not have suggested
anything to write home about but it proved to be the highest score
of the match. It was in fact the first time since England played the
West Indies on a wet wicket in Barbados in 1934–35 that a Test
had not produced a half-century. It was another remarkable
statistic in a summer of remarkable happenings.

Alderman was the Australian bowler who caused us all the
trouble by taking five wickets in the innings, the third time he had
taken five or more on the tour. While he kept going in another one
of those marathon bowling spells which were to become a feature
of the summer, Lillee, Hogg and Bright chipped in with the odd
wicket at the other end.

We started badly when Alderman removed Boycott and
Gower in the space of two overs while the score remained on 29,
and we never recovered. Goochie stayed for a while until he was
caught behind attempting to cut Bright. Gatting helped Mike
Brearley put on 41 for the fourth wicket which proved to be our
highest partnership. I was one of Alderman's five victims, who
cost him just 42 runs off his 23 overs, when I was bowled through
the gate. The knives were no doubt being sharpened in the press
box when the innings folded with 50 minutes of the first day left.
Then those knives had to be blunted a little when Chris Old ran in
to bowl Dyson and have Border caught behind leaving the
Australians on an unhealthy 19 for two at the close.

By the second day there was a little in the pitch for Emburey to

exploit but we were held up by Bright who had come in as
nightwatchman the previous evening. He stayed around too long
for our comfort to make 27 runs. We were also helped as Wood
ran himself out for the umpteenth time when beaten by Old's
direct throw from mid-off.

Thereafter the Australians batted solidly, we defended well,
runs were hard to come by but so were wickets. Hughes and Kent,
making his Test debut, each threatened to beat Mike's top score
by entering the 40s but were then winkled out. Yallop contributed a steady 30. It was nothing to get excited about – at least on
the field – but the impression given on television was that war had
broken out.

That all started when Yallop arrived at the wicket with
Australia 115 for four. He joined his captain who was desperately
trying to hold the innings together against Willis who was desperately trying to tear it apart. After his eight wickets at Headingley
there was always a great cheer when Willis started to bowl on his
home ground. The crowd kept up the chant as he ran towards the
wicket. I've never known such noise and backing for England in a
Test match. It was wonderful stuff which all helped to get us fired
up. It was nothing like the chants of 'kill, kill, kill' that the
Australian fans adopted when Lillee or Jeff Thomson were in full
stride, but it helped to get Willis going.

Yallop went through agony when he first arrived at the crease,
trying to combat Willis who was pitching in the odd short one.
They were never dangerous or intimidating. In fact it was almost a
great feat for Willis to get the ball up chest-high, but he did now
and again to trouble Yallop and have umpire Dickie Bird hopping
around a little, twice talking to his colleague Don Oslear.

The left-handed Yallop was looking so uncomfortable that
Hughes even moved in to protect him, turning down singles in
order to keep Yallop away from Willis. I thought that was ridiculous, taking things much too far. It couldn't have pleased Yallop
too much either because it made him look rather foolish in front
of the crowd. Here was a Test-class batsman playing in his
twenty-ninth Test yet needing the protection of another batsman
on a slowish wicket.

Hughes' action didn't impress Willis too much either. When it
became clear what Hughes was doing Willis let him have two

shortish deliveries in succession. Hughes flayed at the first and missed, flayed at the second and got an edge which streaked between the slips and went for four. As soon as he connected with that ball and had seen it go through the slips Hughes started to run. I gather the television close-up suggested that Hughes was snarling and shouting at Willis who was standing at the end of his follow-through. This led to the suggestion that war had broken out, and feelings were roused. Hughes was having a go all right. Not at Willis but at himself for having played such a streaky shot. As he started on his run he was shouting 'concentrate, concentrate'. There was nothing said in Willis' direction.

There was one other minor incident around the same time, so minor that I didn't even bother to find out what had happened or what had been said. It occurred when Yallop stopped Willis in the middle of his run, walked over and spoke to Mike Gatting who was squatting on his haunches at short square leg a couple of yards away. I can only imagine now that Gatting was giving Yallop a bit of chat but nobody got excited about it. I've often wondered since whether the false impression gained by that television close-up of Hughes apparently having a go at Willis might have given Lillee a false picture and could have explained his action later on, which I thought was a silly one.

Above: Just the breakthrough we wanted. John Emburey supplied the awkward, turning delivery, Graham Yallop supplied the edge as he tried to counter the spin and I supplied the left-handed catch at silly mid-off to end the 58 run fourth-wicket partnership between Yallop and fellow left-hander Allan Border. These two had been threatening to take Australia to their 151 victory target in the fourth Test at Edgbaston

Below: The final day at Edgbaston. This is the moment that paved the way to my five-wicket-for-one-run haul which was to clinch our dramatic 29 run win and put us 2–1 ahead in the series. Allan Border's brave innings of 40 in just under four hours is ended by Mike Gatting taking a superb catch at short-leg off John Emburey's bowling. Bob Taylor and Mike Brearley joined in the celebration. Immediately Border was out I returned to take over the bowling at the other end, the last five wickets going down for 16 runs as I managed to snatch the 'Man of the Match' award again

The first of my five. There can't be a better sight in cricket – for the bowler that is – than seeing a middle stump knocked back. Rodney Marsh was my first victim in my five wickets in 28 deliveries, completely beaten by my yorker as he attempted to drive

Willis was again involved. He bowled one a little bit short to Lillee who took one step backwards towards square leg and steered it over the top of the slips for four runs. He charged up the wicket and caught Willis with what appeared to be a heavy shoulder charge just as Willis was about to turn away and go back to his mark. Lillee claimed afterwards that it was a complete accident, although I must say it didn't look that way to me at the time.

For a start Lillee should not have been within a couple of yards of Willis. Having stepped backwards towards square leg to make room for his stroke and then set off on his run, this should have kept him on the other side of the wicket away from Willis. Instead he ran across the wicket which suggests to me that the 'accidental' collision was not completely innocent. For a second there was an eyeball to eyeball confrontation between two of the world's finest fast bowlers as Willis turned around angrily.

I was accused of getting involved in the incident by having a go at Lillee from second slip when he came back down our end of the wicket. In fact I helped to take the heat out of the situation. 'What kind of shot do you call that?' I shouted to Lillee. 'It's just one of yours from Headingley I've borrowed,' he yelled back. We were both grinning.

He made 18 useful runs during that innings which helped take Australia to 258 and gave them their 69 run lead – leaving us with an awkward hour to get through before the end of the second day.

We coped better than the Australians had the previous evening but suffered the loss of Mike when finishing the day 49 for one, still 20 runs behind. It was a situation which demanded care on the third day, but we overdid it. After the first innings' accusation that we had thrown our wickets away by a succession of careless strokes, we went to the other extreme and hardly put the bat against the ball with any force at all. The result was equally unappetising.

The intervals between the wickets falling seemed fairly lengthy but we failed to make any significant progress in terms of runs. Boycott, Gower and Goochie all got into the twenties and then got out. Gatting managed to reach the thirties before he fell. Willey and I never even managed to get into double figures. My shot was the worst I played in the series. I had made only three when I edged a wildish half-volley well outside the off-stump without moving my feet and gave a catch behind. I knew what was coming when I saw Brian Close bearing down on me as I was having a drink at the end of the day's play. He lectured me then just as he used to lecture me when he was captain of Somerset and I was a youngster just breaking into the side.

By the time I was out, the sixth England wicket to fall, we were only 46 runs on, Boycott, Goochie, Willey and myself having fallen for the addition of just 26 runs. That left Old, Emburey, Taylor and Willis to come. There was not much left in the bank, but the interest produced a handsome profit.

Old started it by helping Gatting stretch the lead to 85 before he was caught behind. Gatting stayed until the lead was 98 before he was bowled by Bright behind his legs attempting to sweep.

Above: It's all over. Another breathtaking victory, England's second in succession. Wicketkeeper Bob Taylor gives a gleeful leap in the air after I bowl Terry Alderman to clinch our staggering 29 run victory. Australia had started their second innings at Edgbaston needing only 151 to win on what was still a fairly good batting wicket. I decided that a straight delivery was all I needed to beat Alderman and so it proved as he obligingly played across the line and missed it completely

Opposite: Earlier at Edgbaston it had been Rodney Marsh's turn to do the leaping about. He claimed the catch behind which dismissed Geoff Boycott and ended the long stay of the Yorkshireman. Boycott's innings had proved invaluable although some critics demanded that he should be sacked for the way he had allowed the Australian bowlers to gain the initiative in our second innings

Then came the highest-scoring partnership of the innings between Emburey and Taylor, exactly 50 for the ninth wicket. It was to prove decisive and to give us new hope and encouragement in the same way Dilley and I had lifted England in the match before. The end soon followed after Alderman had trapped Taylor leg-before and followed up by having Willis caught behind. This left Emburey on 37 not out, his second highest score in Test cricket. But they had given us a chance; Australia now wanted 151 to win, exactly 21 more than they had required at Headingley when they failed.

But this one was going to be much harder to pull off because we could not expect the same amount of help from the conditions as we had received at Headingley. The wicket was helping Emburey turn the ball but it was so slow that the batsman had time to adjust. With so few runs to play with, he couldn't attempt to buy a wicket now and again as spinners like to do. He had to keep it tight, keep the pressure on the batsmen the whole time. Knowing he was likely to prove our match-winner, that he was the one expected to take wickets, it was a nerve-racking time for Emburey.

The Australians had another awkward 40 minute period to get through on that third evening and it proved costly. As on the first evening, Old was the bowler who made the initial breakthrough when he brought one back so sharply that Wood was comprehensively beaten and given out leg-before. He didn't like the decision

---

Above: The most impressive feature of the Australian performances in England during the 1981 summer was their catching. They missed very little and Allan Border provides one example of their handling ability with a diving catch to send back David Gower at Edgbaston.

Below: After failing as an opening batsman, Graham Gooch was dropped down the order for the fourth Test at Edgbaston. But Ray Bright made sure the move did not work when he bowled the Essex man after he had made 21 in England's second innings. Martin Kent looks on and Rodney Marsh is forced to take evasive action to make sure he wasn't hit by a flying bail

and was obviously of the opinion that the ball had done so much it must have been missing leg-stump as well.

With the memory of their collapse at Headingley still so fresh in their minds, the dismissal of Wood must have sent shivers up the backs of the remaining Australian batsmen. They made only nine runs in those final minutes with Border, who had been moved to number three for the Edgbaston Test, opting to play 'doggo'. He was going to be the foundation stone on which Australia could build their victory. By lunchtime on the fourth day he had scored only 13 runs, having then been at the crease for 150 minutes.

Border was going to stick around. His problem was finding someone to stay with him. Only 10 runs had been added on the

When playing the sweep stroke a batsman should always have a pad in the way to provide a second line of defence in case of mishap. Peter Willey failed to provide this and paid the penalty at Edgbaston when he was bowled behind his legs when attempting to sweep Ray Bright

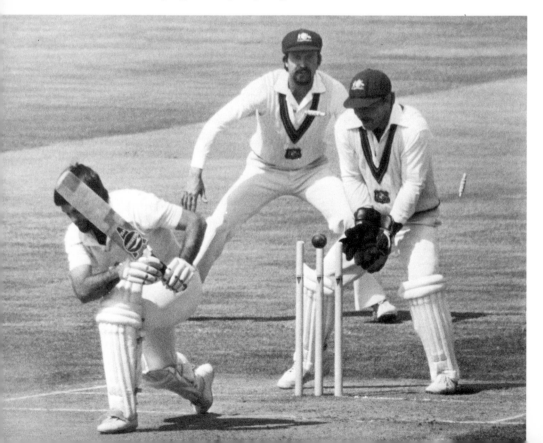

fourth morning when Willis had Dyson leg-before and then tempted Hughes into a hook stroke which sent the ball straight into Emburey's hands on the deep backward square-leg boundary. He was to be crucified for that shot in Australia in the way I had been attacked for my stroke against Viv Richards in Trinidad earlier in the year. Hughes, in fact, hit the ball well.

The partner Border needed arrived at the wicket in the shape of Yallop, although Border himself should have been out before their fourth wicket partnership had started to grow. His concentration had wavered against Willis long enough for him to reach outside his off-stump to a ball slanted across him, but Mike dropped the sharp chance at first slip. Border was not to make

There was no need to look behind me when I was beaten for 26 by Terry Alderman during England's first innings at Edgbaston. As soon as I missed the ball and heard the clunk as it hit the stumps I knew I had been bowled – but I still couldn't help surveying the damage

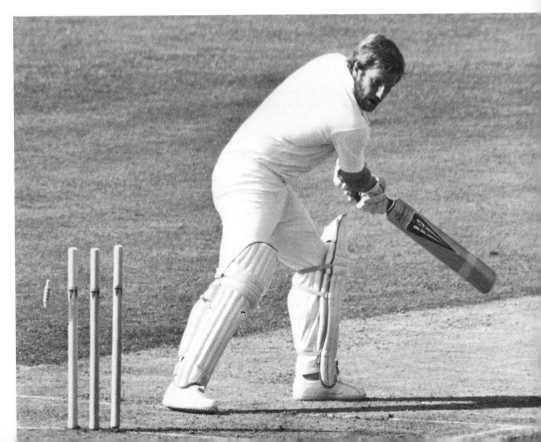

Poor Bob Taylor just couldn't believe it when Australian captain Kim Hughes survived this one during his side's first innings at Edgbaston. Hughes might have been out in two ways. Bob was convinced Hughes was leg-before and then watched the ball go from Hughes's pads just a fraction of an inch past his wicket

---

another mistake until Australia were almost in a position to claim that the match was won. Yallop was just as secure, the two left-handers adding 58 together with Yallop being the more adventurous.

We were relying on Emburey in the main to get rid of them both. Being left-handers he was able to trouble them by pitching into small patches of rough scuffed up by the fast bowlers just outside the off-stump. Strangely it wasn't the rough which got them out in the end. The ball which got Yallop and broke the partnership when Australia were on 87 pitched between the wickets. Yallop tried to turn it away on the onside but got caught out when it turned. It came my way instead at silly mid-off and

When fielding close to the bat at silly mid-off you soon learn to be ready to take quick evasive action. I was ready to get out of the way long before Allan Border actually connected during his second innings of 40 at Edgbaston which almost took his side to victory

lodged into my outstretched left hand.

The incoming Kent, who had looked the best of the Australians in the first innings, was just as obstinate as he helped Border take the score into three figures and reduce the victory target to 46 runs. It was at that stage, with Willis tiring after another astonishing bowling stint, that Mike suggested I should take over and I had persuaded him to use Willey instead.

As I said earlier, there was in fact one more over to come from Emburey, the one that was to claim Border and bring me back into the action. The ball missed the patches of rough but struck another small patch which seemed to crumble on impact, sending up little clouds of dust. It climbed so steeply Border could not

control it. He did manage to play it down but only on to his boot and into Gatting's hands ... I think we knew at that point we had won. I think the Australians knew they had lost it. 'It was amazing, just amazing,' Emburey kept on saying when we raced to congratulate him. 'It just took off, amazing.'

With Border retreating into the pavilion I don't think Mike could have got the ball off me if he had tried. Border was replaced by another left-hander in Marsh who joined with Kent in taking the score to 114 before I managed to strike for the first time. I went round the wicket and bowled him middle-stump as he drove down completely the wrong line. Australia were 114 for six. One more delivery and they were 114 for seven when I had Bright leg-before. It would have knocked down all three wickets.

Lillee was the next to go with the score at 120, falling to the worst ball I bowled and probably the worst ball of the match. I wanted to tempt him into a drive and deliberately set off to deliver it just outside the line of the off-stump, swinging it even further away. In fact I pitched it well outside the off-stump and by the time it passed Lillee he must have had great difficulty in reaching it. But reach it he did which was all that mattered. He got the edge which produced a heart-trembling moment as Taylor moved across to his right, got it into his hands, dropped it, got it again, dropped it once more and finally got it to stick at the third attempt.

Kent was our one remaining worry, but not for long. In my sixth over of that spell I ended his stay when I bowled him between bat

---

Above: Bob Willis makes sure that I taste the victory champagne during the after-match celebrations following our dramatic win at Edgbaston in the fourth Test. I'd just taken the last five Australian wickets for one run and needed the drink. Bowling can be thirsty work!

Below: It's a good job I've got a broad back. In a party mood Geoff Boycott hitches a lift back to the dressing-room after our balcony celebrations at Edgbaston. That victory put us 2–1 ahead in the Ashes series

England v. Australia

WARWICKSHIRE COUNTY CRICKET CLUB.

4th   TEST MATCH

at Edgbaston on

JULY 30th, 31st, AUGUST 1st, 2nd & 3rd 1981

A new ball may be taken after
85 overs

ENGLAND	1st Innings		2nd Innings		AUSTRALIA	1st Innings		2nd Innings	
1. G. BOYCOTT	c Marsh b A'man	13	c Marsh b B'ht	29	1. G.M. WOOD	run out	38	lbw b Old	2
2. J.M. BREARLEY *	c Border b Lillee	48	lbw b Lillee	13	2. J. DYSON	b Old	1	lbw b Willis	13
3. D.I. GOWER	c Hogg b A'man	0	c Border b B'ht	23	3. M. KENT	c Willis b Emburey	46	b Botham	10
4. G.A. GOOCH	c Marsh b Bright	21	b Bright	21	4. K.J. HUGHES *	lbw b Old	47	c E'ey b Willis	5
5. M.W. GATTING	c A'man b Lillee	21	b Bright	39	5. G. YALLOP	b Emburey	30	c Botham b 'ry	30
6. P. WILLEY	b Bright	16	b Bright	5	6. A.R. BORDER	c Taylor b Old	2	c G'ng b E'ry	40
7. I.T. BOTHAM	b Alderman	26	c Marsh b Lillee	3	7. R.W. MARSH +	b Emburey	2	b Botham	4
8. R.W. TAYLOR +	b Alderman	0	lbw b Alderman	8	8. R.J. BRIGHT	lbw b Botham	27	lbw b Botham	0
9. J.E. EMBUREY	b Hogg	3	not out	37	9. D.K. LILLEE	b Emburey	18	c T'or b B'ham	3
10. G.M. OLD	not out	11	c Marsh b A'man	23	10. T. ALDERMAN	not out	3	b Botham	0
11. R.G.D. WILLIS	c Marsh b A'man	13	c Marsh b A'man	2	11. R.M. HOGG	run out	0	not out	0
	Extras	17	Extras	16		Extras	44	Extras	14
	TOTAL	189	TOTAL	219		TOTAL	258	TOTAL	121

1 wkt for- 29 2- 29 3- 60 4-101 5-126 6-145 7- 161 8-161 9- 165 10- 189   1 wkt for 5   2- 14   3- 62   4-115 5- 156 6- 203 7 220 8-253 9- 253 10- 258

1 wkt for- 10 2- 52 3- 89 4- 93 5- 110 6- 115 7-154 8- 167 9-217 10- 219   1 wkt for 2 2- 19 3- 29 4- 87 5-105 6-114 7-114 8-120 9- 121 10-121

* Captain
+ Wicketkeeper

UMPIRES H.D. BIRD, D.O. OSLEAR.
SCORERS C.W. GROVE, D. SHERWOOD.

Bowling Analysis	O	M	R	W	O	M	R	W	Bowling Analysis	O	M	R	W	O	M	R	W
Lillee	18	4	61	2	26	9	51	2	Willis	19	3	63	0	20	6	37	2
Alderman	23.1	8	42	5	22	5	65	3	Old	21	8	44	3	11	4	19	1
Hogg	16	3	49	1	10	3	19	0	Emburey	26.5	12	43	4	22	10	40	2
Bright	12	4	20	2	34	17	68	5	Botham	20	1	64	1	13	9	11	5

ENGLAND   won the toss and elected to BAT.

HOURS OF PLAY

1st 3 days.		4th day	12noon – 7.00p.m.	5th day	11.00a.m. – 5.30 or 6.00p.m.
LUNCH	1.30p.m. – 2.10p.m.	LUNCH	2.00p.m. – 2.40p.m.	LUNCH	1.00p.m. – 1.40p.m.
TEA	4.10p.m. – 4.30p.m.	TEA	4.40p.m. – 5.00p.m.	TEA	3.40p.m. – 4.00p.m.

1st 3 days. 11.30 a.m. – 6.30p'm.

ENGLAND WON BY 29 RUNS.

and pad with the score on 121 for nine. With the last ball of that over I bowled Alderman as well, so in 28 deliveries I had taken five wickets for the cost of only one run. Australia were beaten by 29 runs, England were now 2–1 up in the series.

At Headingley I had been voted Cornhill's 'Man of the Match' by Fred Trueman who had described my runs and wickets as a 'captain's performance one match too late'. I had thought I stood a chance of that award, but I was a little surprised when Trevor Bailey made me Cornhill's 'Man of the Match' at Edgbaston for those last five wickets. I really had not expected that. I'm not complaining mind you. But I thought John Emburey might have qualified for his four wickets in the first innings, his two decisive wickets in the second in getting rid of Border and Yallop plus his unbeaten 37 which had really made all the difference.

So, for the third weekend in succession I was drinking victory champagne. First at Headingley, then at Lord's where a splendid bowling performance by Joel Garner followed by yet another century by Viv Richards had beaten Surrey in the Benson and Hedges Cup Final to give Somerset the trophy. Now at Edgbaston, where the celebrations went on long into the night at a benefit dinner that had been arranged for Bob Willis. The timing couldn't have been better.

8 The greatest ever -fifth Test

Following their Edgbaston defeat the Australians were being labelled 'Kim's Kamikaze Kids' back home. One Australian critic went on to say: 'They showed about as much character as a melting chocolate ice cream.' Hysterical demands were made for Greg Chappell to drop everything in order to fly to England and take charge. It wasn't as bad as that.

Our victory at Headingley was a cricketing fluke. Kim Hughes had said after the match: 'We had done everything right except win it.' You can't legislate for freak results. Their performance at Edgbaston hadn't been particularly inspired, but the captaincy of Mike Brearley must not be overlooked when looking for reasons why Australia collapsed so dramatically in their second innings.

Mike's field placings on that last day had been magnificent. I don't recall him missing a single trick. With so few runs to play with yet needing to take wickets regularly, the situation is very tricky. If you keep fielders up around the bat to take the catches you give batsmen undeserved runs, which always upsets the bowler. Spread the field out to stop the runs and you miss the chance of taking the catches which could swing the match your way.

The way Mike set the field he was able to do both. He was able to put pressure on the batsmen and fill them with fear and trepidation even when he permitted himself only four fielders in close catching positions and had the rest spread almost around the boundary. The batsmen found their most productive scoring strokes were blocked everywhere they looked. It must have appeared that England had twice as many fielders out there as they should have done. It was an object-lesson in the art of field placing, one I shall never forget.

At Old Trafford for the fifth Test Mike was due to be leading

England for the final time: he had come to the end of his three-match appointment. If he turned out to be successful again, which would mean England keeping the Ashes with an uncatchable 3–1 series lead, his mission would be complete. The selectors could then choose another captain for the final Test at the Oval and use it to try out the man who would be leading England in India during the winter.

The rest of the team did not want it to be the end for Mike at Old Trafford, whatever the outcome of the Test match. I think the selectors caught our mood. Before the Old Trafford Test started there was already a hint from them that they would give him the final Test as well to allow him to bow out in full glory after the staggering job he had done. I didn't want him to go. In fact I made several attempts to talk him into making himself available for India as well. But he was adamant that he couldn't afford the time.

When Rodney Hogg was first introduced to Mike he remarked: 'You're the guy who has got a degree in people aren't you?' That just about sums Mike up. He has also described our relationship as one of me needing a father figure and him needing a younger brother. 'We just seem to be good for each other.'

I like to think I am good for him. We are vastly different types with vastly differing tastes. Although we enjoy each other's company, we do not spend a great deal of time together away from the cricket field. He is certainly good for me. He has a go at me now and again, telling me to back off when I get too carried away, but he generally lets me have my head. When Mike is in charge you feel you want to do everything possible to make sure he comes out the winner. I know the other players feel exactly the same.

We all went to Old Trafford determined to demonstrate to the cricketing public – and their numbers had been swollen by many thousands after our victories in the previous two Tests – that we were the better side. That the Ashes would stay in England's care because we had earned them and not because of one fluke and one miracle. I think we did just that.

This determination also applied to the three new members of the side who had not previously played in the Ashes series that summer. They were the Kent pairing of Chris Tavare and Alan

Knott, who were coming back into Test cricket, and new arrival Paul Allott, who was making his debut because injury had once again struck down Chris Old and because a strange misunderstanding about the wicket had made the call-up of a third Kent player, left-arm spinner Derek Underwood, a waste of time.

To make room for Tavare's return and in an attempt to add some measure of stability to our batting, Peter Willey had been sacrificed. I felt very sorry for him. He had been my sergeant-major in the West Indies, and I could not have wished for a better one. Tough, a man of few words who doesn't stand any nonsense, he gets as bitter and upset at defeat in a Test match as Bob Willis. He was greatly respected by all the players. One word from Willey was enough to bring them to order if some became a little too carried away with fun and games in the dressing-room.

Willey had waited a long time before finishing up on a winning England side. He liked the feeling. He liked it even more when we won two Test matches in a row. Then came the axe. His reaction was typical: 'When are we due to play the West Indies again? Perhaps I'll get another chance then.'

I felt even more sympathy for him the following day, even if I didn't show it in the best possible way. Somerset were playing Northamptonshire at Weston the weekend that Willey was dropped, the announcement being made on the Sunday. On the Monday I was bowling to him in the Championship match when I broke his thumb, which was to keep him out of first-class cricket for almost a month. It was a sorry twenty-four hours.

The other main change had been the recall of Alan Knott behind the wicket for Bob Taylor. This move was largely influenced by the conditions the selectors expected to find at Old Trafford when they sat down to pick the team. Alec Bedser had made a careful check earlier in the week and was told that the wicket would be similar to the one at Edgbaston, with perhaps a little more bounce and expected to help the spinners over the last couple of days. With that in mind the selectors had called in Underwood to help Emburey in the spinning department. They planned to go into the match with five bowlers – myself included – instead of four as we had been using previously. Our batting being what it was, they also opted for Knotty's greater run-scoring potential over Taylor's.

With his batting potential to support his outstanding wicketkeeping ability, I've always regarded Alan Knott as the number one choice in the England side. My first move as England captain was to seek his recall to Test cricket in 1980. Here Knotty gets in some practice at Old Trafford when Mike Brearley asked for him to help clinch the 1981 Ashes series

The composition of the side might have been different if somebody had bothered to tell the selectors that the Test wicket had been left exposed to the thunderstorms which drenched Manchester on the Thursday. It was not until two days after the team had been announced that Alec Bedser learned from a cricket writer that the square at Old Trafford had been under water for a while and the wicket would not be as they expected. That takes me back to my earlier point about the Test and County Cricket Board having complete charge of all Test match arrangements in this country.

The Australians were also having their team troubles. In

Leg-side catches are never the easiest for wicketkeepers to take. For part of the time the ball is obscured by the batsman's body and there is only a split second to pick up the flight again. Alan Knott makes it look so easy in dismissing Ray Bright off Bob Willis' bowling during the final day at Old Trafford

addition to Lawson being unavailable, Hogg had broken down again which left them a fast bowler short. Their first choice reserve had been Carl Rackemann, a tall right-arm fast bowler from Queensland who had played against us for his state when we toured there in 1979–80 and was in England having a few games for Surrey's second eleven. But he, too, was injured. They turned instead to Mike Whitney, a twenty-two-year-old left-arm fast bowler from New South Wales who was in England playing for Fleetwood in the Northern League and had been signed up by Gloucestershire. That day he had been selected to make his Schweppes Championship debut against Hampshire at Cheltenham when Gloucestershire received the Australians' SOS. They immediately pulled him out of the match, although it had started, and sent him racing to Manchester. It was the start of twenty-four hours he will certainly never forget.

Tavare will never forget his return to Test cricket either. Allott will forever remember the first time he picked up a bat for England. But I don't think the rest of us will want to recall England's first innings in a hurry, except perhaps Boycott. I personally have no wish to remember it as I was out first ball.

Boycott didn't last long when Mike chose to bat first: he made only 10 runs. But those 10 were sufficient to take him past Colin Cowdrey's record aggregate for England and make Boycott the most prolific Test batsman we have produced. Now only Sir Gary Sobers stands ahead of him in the world. It was a great relief to all of us when Boycott turned Alderman to the boundary to make sure of beating Cowdrey.

Boycott had said on several occasions that he didn't go out chasing records but I had a feeling that this one had bothered him throughout the series. He had been within striking distance of going into the lead when the first Test match started but it had taken him until the fifth Test to go ahead. I thought he would be all the better for getting it out of his system.

Apart from an innings of 23 by Gower and another of 32 from Gatting, the story of our first innings of 231 can be told by the exploits of two men, Tavare and Allott. Tavare went in on the stroke of noon, when Boycott was out, and stayed there until 10 minutes before the close, ignoring boos, jeers and slow handclaps in making his 69 runs. I often fail to understand the crowds at cricket matches. Maybe Tavare's long, slow innings was not what they had come to see after the thrills and spills of the previous two Test matches, particularly at Old Trafford where, I gather, limited-over cricket dominates the thoughts of the supporters.

Personally, I don't think I could ever bat as Tavare did that day and was to do later in the match. I'm just not made that way. But there has to be somebody in the side who is capable of playing as he did. England would have been in a great mess without him and it was sickening to hear the crowd having a go at him when he needed praising and encouraging.

Tavare watched Goochie, Gower, Gatting, Brearley, myself,

Knott and Emburey go before he found somebody to outlast him in Allott coming in at number 10. He had then made 40 – at one stage of the day he had been stuck at 12 for a period of 45 minutes – but the danger of running out of partners caused him to put on a spurt. His last 50 minutes at the crease brought him an additional 29 runs before he edged a catch to first slip and gave Whitney his second wicket.

If Tavare had worried about Allott's ability to stay around the crease, he need not have done. Allott had made just nine when he started again on the second morning but he stayed around to mark his Test debut with an unbeaten 52 – a career best – much to the delight of a packed Old Trafford ground. And our delight too. Without him we would never have got beyond the 200 mark.

But even that was not the end of his contribution to England's cause on an amazing second day which saw the Australians bowled out in two and a half hours off just 30 overs. This was the occasion when their batting could have been described as being as characterless as melting ice cream, the effort made by Kent being the one exception.

Once again it was Willis who undermined them with an astonishing third over during which he took the wickets of Dyson, Hughes and Yallop. It was extraordinary. Dyson went off the first ball when he gave me a simple catch at third slip. Hughes then produced the shot of a desperate man when he sent the first ball he received crashing through the covers for four, but he was leg-before to the fourth ball. Finally Yallop gave me my second easy slip catch off the final delivery.

That left Australia 24 for three. One ball later they were 24 for four when Allott claimed his first Test victim by having Wood leg-before. Their innings was virtually all over bar the shouting.

Opposite: You probably won't find this stroke in any cricket coaching manual but Paul Allott doesn't care. It proved effective enough on this occasion to help Lancashire's medium-paced bowler celebrate his Test call-up at Old Trafford with a career best of an unbeaten 52 in our first innings 231. Paul impressed me immensely by the way he quickly settled down and he seems booked to fill the role played by Chris Old and Mike Hendrick in the England side for some years to come

Kent did his best to hold the side together with another impressive innings which brought him 52 runs. Bright struck 22 runs as the tail was falling apart. They were all out for 130 which gave us a first innings lead of 101 – far beyond our wildest dreams. There was just no explanation for their startling collapse. Except that we took all our catches, for once, in support of good bowling.

This was our chance to really make our presence felt and squeeze all life out of the Australians. We came close to messing it up until I managed to produce an innings of which I shall always be proud. It even commanded a third of the front page of *The Times* asking whether it might have been 'the greatest Test innings ever played'. That's for other people to judge. I was just grateful for the chance of helping England out of a hole after we had slipped to 104 for five on a wicket getting better.

We had started the day at 70 for one but then lost four wickets in producing another 34 runs, which let the Australians in with a chance when all their hopes should have been killed off. Once again Tavare had held firm, scoring only 11 runs in the two hours 20 minutes he had been at the crease when I walked out to join him.

It wasn't a Headingley situation again. I had walked out there when the match was seemingly lost which gave me the freedom to strike out with gay abandon knowing I had nothing to lose. At Old Trafford we were in danger of throwing the match away. I had to pick my shots and my moments. But I was deeply conscious of the fact that the new ball wasn't far away and that I needed to have my

Above: I must have given the Australian slip fielders plenty of food for thought during my barnstorming century at Old Trafford. Here Graeme Wood, Allan Border, Terry Alderman and John Dyson are caught in reflective mood, each one no doubt wondering how they would attempt to get me out if they were in charge!

Below: Even Kim Hughes, Australia's captain, scratches his head searching for inspiration after I had launched my attack on the Australian new ball during my century at Old Trafford. I brought my innings to an end myself with an ill-judged attempted steer against Mike Whitney which ended up in Rodney Marsh's gloves

eye in by the time it arrived – if I could last out that long.

To have Tavare at the other end and playing as securely as he was, proved a tremendous help. I didn't have to worry about the Australians making a breakthrough there, and that left me free to concentrate entirely on my own game. I played myself in quietly. I don't think I missed a scoring opportunity when it arose, but I didn't take a chance either. I've since read that in the 65 minutes I spent at the crease before the arrival of the new ball, I faced 59 deliveries off which I scored 28 runs.

I was completely ready for the new ball when Alderman took it as soon as it was due, Lillee sharing it at the other end. Everything just went sweetly from that moment onwards. I didn't deliberately set out to take the Australian attack apart. At the same time I was determined they were not going to dominate me. If the ball was there to be hit then I was going to hit it. When Lillee dropped it short, as he did in sheer exasperation, I was going to hook it. It was not until I saw a television re-run of my innings later that I realised I twice hooked him off my eyebrows for six. If I had missed either shot the ball would have caught me right in the middle of the forehead each time. Perhaps that was the reason I connected so well – out of sheer self-preservation.

As far as the actual details of my innings are concerned I've had to rely on the statisticians. I understand that just before I warmed up, Tavare reached his half-century in 306 minutes (which was the slowest half-century ever scored in a Test match in England). I

Above: Kim Hughes appears to be offering up a little prayer as he calls up Australia's left-arm fast bowler Mike Whitney to bowl at me during my century at Old Trafford. Kim obviously feared the worst after the way I had dealt with Dennis Lillee and Terry Alderman, but Whitney was to claim my wicket in the end to celebrate his first Test cap

Below: Allan Border, Australia's stocky, middle order left-handed batsman, looks puzzled as to how he managed to reach his century during his side's second innings at Old Trafford. I can tell him. It was by a thoroughly courageous and professional performance which was the mark of most of his innings against us during the 1981 summer. He caused us more concern than almost the rest of the Australian batting put together, even though he batted with a broken finger in his left hand on this occasion

also gather that I went from 28 when the new ball was taken to my century in just another 27 deliveries, reaching three figures with a sweep for six against Bright which went over Lillee's head at long-leg. That was after the break for tea which came when I was on 94.

I wasn't to stay around for long afterwards. There was time to drive Bright straight for another six, the sixth of my innings to add to my 13 fours. It was, apparently, the first time that six sixes had ever been scored in an Ashes Test innings in this country, which I find rather remarkable considering some of the huge scores that have been produced.

In fact all sorts of interesting statistics popped up as a result of my 118 scored out of the 149 Tavare and I put on for the sixth wicket in 123 minutes. My century was only one delivery quicker than the one I had scored at Headingley but it was 15 deliveries slower than the fastest recorded in Test cricket, that of Roy Fredericks for the West Indies against Australia in Perth in 1975 which occupied only 71 deliveries. Against that I did move slightly faster than Fredericks in part of my innings when I went from five to 118 in 70 deliveries. Not that I get particularly excited about such things, although many people find them fascinating.

I remember feeling pretty shattered when I eventually got back to the dressing-room after attempting to cut Whitney and edging a catch to Marsh. Most of the breath had been knocked out of me by the back slaps I'd received as I pushed my way through the crowd at the end of it all. There were more waiting for me in the dressing-room. But the most pleasing thing about it all was that I had managed to take the wind out of the Australian sails.

When I left the crease Tavare soldiered steadily on, taking two minutes over seven hours to make his 78, while Knott signalled his return to Test cricket with a lively 59 and Emburey followed up his Edgbaston display with the bat by making his first half-century in Tests. When our second innings ended on the Sunday we had made 404 which gave us a 505 run lead. We were never going to be beaten, although the Australians made a brave attempt to draw the match.

Graham Yallop and Allan Border, who showed immense courage in batting with a finger broken when he attempted to take a slip catch in our innings, were the two players who threatened to delay the outcome of the Ashes series until the final match at The Oval. They each made centuries, and Yallop's innings was the most polished I have seen him produce.

Any serious thoughts the Australians may have entertained of being able to bat out the remaining 10 hours – or even winning the game – were virtually ruined by a mindless piece of cricket soon after the start of their second innings when Dyson was run out. In Willis' second over Dyson pushed the ball out into the covers away from Gower and started off for a single which should have been there. Wood responded, but changed his mind when Dyson was over halfway. Dyson never stood a chance of making all that ground a second time to beat Gower's accurate return.

Wood was not to prosper long after his error of judgment, flicking at a long hop from Allott and giving Knotty a leg-side catch of the type he swallows with considerable ease, although many other wicketkeepers would have put it down. Hughes was the first Australian batsman to threaten us when joining with Yallop in a 95 run partnership for the third wicket before I got one through his guard and was rewarded with my leg-before appeal.

Then our worries started to increase. Yallop settled down quite comfortably on a now perfect batting wicket and went on to make his third century against England, his sixth in all, in a stay of 177 minutes. We were glad to see the back of him when he was bowled by Emburey by one that kept low. Before the close of play Kent was to fall as well, leaving the Australians on 210 for five, another six hours to survive to draw the game, another 296 required if they were going to win it.

I never thought they had a chance of doing either, but we all became a little concerned as under Border's influence the minutes ticked away and the runs required were steadily ticked off. He had considerable assistance from Marsh and Lillee: Marsh had not made much of an impact with the bat in the series and there was always the chance that he would come good some day. He was almost good enough that final day, but not quite good enough to deal with Willis who eased our concern by having both him and Bright caught behind.

That still left Lillee to deal with as the fast bowler joined Border in a 51 run partnership which took Australia to 373.

Fortunately I put an end to his presence when taking a two-handed catch high to my right at slip. The end was not far away.

Alderman was no problem. We fancied taking his wicket any time. We also fancied a quick dismissal of Whitney if he was batting behind Alderman but he gave us more trouble than we expected. Not in terms of runs scored: he didn't manage one during his hour at the crease. But he kept Border company while the Australians took their score to 402 before he was caught at short-leg off Willis. Even then he was reluctant to go, only dragging himself away from the crease when the rest of us – Border included – raced away in an effort to beat the masses swarming over the boundary fence ready for the end-of-match presentations. For the third match in succession I was made 'Man of the Match', but the vital statistic was the one which showed we had won by 103 runs to make sure of the Ashes.

I found it all a little embarrassing afterwards – and I'm not easily embarrassed. Congratulations were still pouring in following my century on the Saturday, two days earlier, while Mike Brearley was likening me to Dr W. G. Grace. I wasn't quite sure how to take that. I'm not a dainty figure but even I can't match the Doctor for size. And I'd never sport a beard as shaggy as his!

That wasn't quite the end of my fast-scoring feats for the season. I rather overindulged myself the following Sunday when playing for Somerset in the John Player League match against Hampshire at Taunton. It was one of the few occasions when I have even managed to put Viv Richards in the shade. I scored a century that day in only 67 minutes. My second 50 was officially timed as taking just nine minutes, although many people swear that seven minutes was more like it. And all the time Viv was at the wicket watching me as together we put on 179 in 67 minutes for the fifth wicket, the highest fifth-wicket partnership in any form of limited-over cricket.

Everything just went right for me in hitting seven sixes and nine fours. At one stage I remember looking at the scoreboard and seeing Viv in the eighties while I had 40 or so. He was still in the eighties when I reached my century. How did I manage to outscore Viv? That's easy. I can count better than he can and knew when the sixth ball was coming up so that I could sneak the single to make sure I kept the strike.

England won the toss and elected to bat

England won by 103 runs

FIFTH TEST MATCH
OLD TRAFFORD

England v. Australia

ENGLAND

Thursday 13th, August
Friday 14th, August
Saturday, 15th, August
    11.30 - 6.30 or [7.30]
Sunday 16th, August
    12.00 - 7.00 or [8.00]
Monday 17th, August
    11.00 - 5.30 or 6.00

	First Innings		Second Innings	
1 G. BOYCOTT	c Marsh b Alderman	10	lbw Alderman	37
2 G. A. GOOCH	lbw Lillee	10	b Alderman	5
3 C. J. TAVARE	c Alderman b Whitney	69	c Kent b Alderman	78
4 D. I. GOWER	c Yallop b Whitney	23	c Bright b Lillee	1
* 5 J. M. BREARLEY	lbw Alderman	2	c Marsh b Alderman	3
6 I. T. BOTHAM	c Bright b Lillee	0	c Marsh b Whitney	118
† 7 A. P. E KNOTT	c Border b Alderman	13	c Dyson b Lillee	59
8 J. E. EMBUREY	c Border b Alderman	1	c Kent b Whitney	57
9 P. J. W. ALLOTT	not out	52	c Hughes b Bright	14
10 M. W. GATTING	c Border b Lillee	32	lbw Alderman	11
11 R. G. D. WILLIS	c Hughes b Lillee	11	not out	5
	Ex. bs. 6 lb. 2 wds. nb.	8	Ex. 1 bs. 12 lb. wds. 3 nb.	16
	Total	231	Total	404

FALL OF WICKETS

First Innings		Second Innings	
1 - 19		1 - 7	
2 - 25		2 - 79	
3 - 57		3 - 80	
4 - 62		4 - 98	
5 -109		5 -104	
6 -109		6 -253	
7 -131		7 -282	
8 -132		8 -356	
9 -175		9 -396	

BOWLING ANALYSIS

	O	M	R	W	Wds.	NBs.	O	M	R	W	Wds.	NBs.
Lillee	24.1	8	55	4	...		46	13	137	2	...	1
Alderman	29	5	88	4	2		52	19	109	5	...	2
Whitney	17	3	50	2	...		27	6	74	2	...	...
Bright	16	6	30	0	...		26.4	12	68	1	...	...

LUNCH INTERVALS

Thurs, Fri, Sat,
    1.30 - 2.10
Sunday 2.00 2.40
Monday 1.00 - 1.40

TEA INTERVALS

Thurs, Fri, Sat,
    4.10 - 4.30
Sunday 4.40 - 5.00
Monday 3.40 - 4.00

AUSTRALIA

	First Innings		Second Innings	
1 G. WOOD	lbw Allott	19	c Knott b Allott	6
2 M. F. KENT	c Knott b Emburey	52	c Brearley b Emburey	2
* 3 K. J. HUGHES	lbw Willis	4	lbw Botham	43
4 G. N. YALLOP	c Botham b Willis	0	b Emburey	114
5 J. DYSON	c Botham b Willis	0	run out	5
6 A. R. BORDER	c Gower b Botham	11	not out	123
† 7 R. W. MARSH	c Botham b Willis	1	c Knott b Willis	47
8 R. J. BRIGHT	c Knott b Botham	22	c Knott b Willis	5
9 T. M. ALDERMAN	not out	2	lbw Botham	0
10 D. K. LILLEE	c Gooch b Botham	13	c Botham b Allott	28
11 M. R. WHITNEY	b Allott	0	c Gatting b Willis	0
12 T. M. CHAPPELL	Ex. bs. lb. wds. 6 nb.	6	Ex. bs. 9 lb. 2 wds. 18 nb.	29
	Total	130	Total	402

FALL OF WICKETS

First Innings		Second Innings	
1 - 20		1 - 7	
2 - 24		2 - 24	
3 - 24		3 -119	
4 - 24		4 -198	
5 - 58		5 -206	
6 - 59		6 -296	
7 -104		7 -322	
8 -125		8 -373	
9 -126		9 -378	

BOWLING ANALYSIS

	O	M	R	W	Wds.	NBs.	O	M	R	W	Wds.	NBs.
Willis	14	0	63	4	...	6	30.5	2	96	3	...	15
Allott	6	1	17	2	...	...	17	3	71	2	...	...
Botham	6.2	1	28	3	...	...	36	16	86	2	2	1
Emburey	4	0	16	1	...	...	49	9	107	2	...	...
Gatting							3	1	13	0	...	2

Umpires:

D. J. Constant, & K. E. Palmer.

*Captain †Wicket Keeper

9 Farewell to Mike Brearley
- sixth Test

I don't think anybody – officials, selectors, cricket writers or the general public – realised how much the winter tour of the West Indies took out of the players who went there and played regularly in the Test series. But the evidence was there for everybody to see in the make-up of the England side for the final Test of the Ashes series.

There was no Graham Gooch, no David Gower or Peter Willey in the batting line-up. No Paul Downton behind the wicket. No Graham Dilley to supply the bowling spearhead. Of the players who had featured regularly in the Test series in the Caribbean, only Geoff Boycott, John Emburey and myself remained to appear at The Oval. The rest had fallen by the wayside. There had also been a demand that Boycott should not be included.

After our return from the Caribbean we had had less than a week's rest before joining our respective county clubs to start the domestic season – a season that is much tougher now than it has ever been, even though we may play less cricket than players did 30 or 40 years ago. A programme of 28 – or even 32 – championship matches is far less demanding mentally and physically than our present jumbled-up season where we are constantly switching from one form of cricket to another. Five hours of John Player League cricket on a Sunday afternoon can drain you far quicker than a championship match spread over three days.

On more than one occasion during the summer both Graham Gooch and David Gower told me they felt absolutely shattered. I'm sure this sheer exhaustion was the reason for their lack of success in the Ashes series and not because they were suffering from a lack of form. They were so exhausted mentally they found it difficult to concentrate. Against a county side they were able to get away with it, as Goochie demonstrated when he finished the season hitting centuries galore. Against a series of top-class bowlers coming at you all the time as happened when playing against Australia, one momentary lapse of concentration often proves fatal.

That is the only reason I can offer to explain why Goochie finished the Test match at Old Trafford having made just 139 from 10 visits to the crease in the Ashes series. One of those visits brought him 44 runs at Lord's. Or why Gower should have made only 250 runs from 10 innings, including one innings of 89. Or why Boycott had made only 255 runs from a similar number of outings.

If there is any other explanation behind those modest returns I haven't come across it. Whatever the reason, the selectors now took the opportunity – with the Ashes retained – of resting Goochie and Gower, making room for the reintroduction of Wayne Larkins and the promotion of Sussex's Paul Parker for his Test debut. They wanted to study them both with the tour of India in mind.

One other change was made in the team with Mike Hendrick returning in place of Allott who became twelfth man. It was intended that Allott's place should go to Chris Old but he broke down in the final net session after damaging a thigh muscle playing for Yorkshire. The injury jinx had struck him down once more, leaving him with a record which was to tell against him, I understand, when the tour party to India was selected. The Australians just made the one change in their last attempt to restore some of the country's cricketing pride: Dirk Welham stepped in for his Test debut in place of John Dyson and Kent was promoted to opener.

Sadly, the match proved to be a bit of an anti-climax after all that had gone before. I say sadly because the public responded magnificently to our three successive victories by flocking to The Oval in their thousands, resulting in many being locked out on each of the first three days. It's disappointing having to turn so many away from a cricket match after long periods of trying to get the public out of their armchairs and into the grounds again.

I think we were all a little bit battle-weary after the summer we'd had which probably explained Australia's 120 run start when they were put in. It was the right decision for Mike to make in his farewell appearance as England captain. The Test was being played on one of the new Oval wickets. It was rock hard, a credit to groundsman Harry Brind, and offered pace and bounce to the quicker bowlers. We were just unable to exploit it.

The match was well into the first afternoon before I managed our first breakthrough. It proved to be a double strike with Wood and Kent falling within five runs of each other, although it didn't help us to make serious inroads into the Australian batting. Wood was the first to go. He changed his mind after he had started to go for a hook shot but could not get his bat out of the way in time to avoid a top edge which gave Mike a catch at first slip. In my next over I had Kent checking an attempted off-drive and leaving Gatting to take the catch at mid-off.

We didn't have much joy during the remainder of the day, except for the strange dismissal of Hughes. He was the third of the six wickets with which I was to finish. The ball was short, just right for the pull-shot Hughes played but his back foot slipped as he made the stroke and dislodged the leg-side bail. Hughes had completed his second run before he realised what had happened. The only other wicket to fall was that of Yallop while Border dug

---

Above: Mike Brearley doesn't look too happy at getting out during his second innings of the final Test at The Oval but there is no reason why he shouldn't be. In what is expected to be his last innings for England he had saved his side from possible defeat with a defiant half-century. After all that Mike has done for me I was delighted for him. Australian captain Kim Hughes doesn't look too happy either. He knew, by then, that Australia's hopes of salvaging some of their reputation with a last-gasp victory had disappeared by the time Mike had edged a catch behind

Below: Alec Bedser has taken more than his fair share of stick during his thirteen-year reign as chairman of selectors. Nobody has worked harder in trying to build a winning England side. Even with the Ashes retained, Alec still looks worried during the after-match presentation ceremony at The Oval following the final Test. Perhaps he was still thinking of his last duty as chairman – picking the England squad for the winter tour of India. Whatever the reason for his look, Alec must have known he bowed out respected by every player who served him

Opposite above: It is not all fun playing cricket. It hurts a little as well as I discovered at The Oval during the final Test. I pinched a nerve low in my spine which caused me agony every time I put my left foot on the ground whilst bowling 89 overs in the match. My grimace was even enough to prompt Geoff Boycott to offer a word in sympathy

Opposite below: The Australian close fielders might have found it painful too if they had got in the way of this full-blooded stroke from Mike Brearley during his half-century in England's second innings. They were wise enough to scatter as Mike made sure his four-match comeback as England leader was not marred by defeat

This page: I never had any doubts that Geoff Boycott would score a century in the final Test at The Oval. He hadn't scored a century before during the series which was one good reason why I thought he would succeed at the final hurdle. Calls were also being made for his head so that he could be replaced by a younger player on the tour of India. That was another good reason. Boycott didn't let me down and not even this attempted stumping by Rodney Marsh off Ray Bright could put the Yorkshireman off his dedicated path towards his 137

himself in again on his way to his second unbeaten century, which he was to complete on the second day with last man Whitney at the wicket.

By the end of that first day Australia had scored 251 for four and our own troubles were beginning to mount up. I had started the match with a suspect left knee which meant that I couldn't bound up to the wicket in the way I had been doing over the last three Test matches. I would have got away with it under normal circumstances but I suddenly found myself carrying an extra burden when Willis damaged some stomach muscles and Hendrick strained his side. Both of them had to be used sparingly.

The result of their injuries meant that I had to wind myself up on the second day and keep myself going like a piece of clockwork in getting through a 21 over spell bowling unchanged from the pavilion end for 10 minutes short of three hours. It was not without some measure of reward in that the long spell enabled me to finish with six wickets, even though my 47 overs in the innings cost me 125 runs.

Once Welham had been bowled by Willis the rest went fairly quickly, exposing Border to the danger of running out of partners before he had had a chance of making his second successive century. He was still 20 runs away when Whitney arrived at the crease to join him. As in the second innings at Old Trafford he managed to stay around while Border climbed into three figures after batting 275 minutes. This time Whitney even managed to score. He showed more joy over his first run in Test cricket than Border had done over his century. He was so pleased with himself that his display of sheer delight prompted Border to walk down

---

It's that man Border again. A shortish delivery, a heave from those powerful shoulders of his and yet another four at The Oval on his way to his second century in successive Test innings. He followed his unbeaten 123 at Old Trafford with an undefeated 106 at The Oval and was to spend just over 15 hours at the crease in three innings before we took his wicket. His performances at The Oval were to restore his Test match average to above 50 which makes him one of the leading batsmen in the world today

the wicket and shake Whitney's hand in congratulations. And calm him down at the same time!

By the time Whitney had become my final victim when playing completely down the wrong line and missing a fairly straight delivery, Australia had made 352. A careful and studied reply was required from us if we were not to fall flat on our faces at the last hurdle. It was just the situation Boycott revels in.

He doesn't often miss out by not scoring a century in a Test series, and he knew he was under a bit of pressure as well. At the age of 40 many people were beginning to ask whether it wasn't time for him to step aside and make way for a younger opening batsman. But people have been saying that about Boycott for years and he was not going to give up his England place without a struggle. And struggle he had to against Lillee who was probably making his last Test appearance in England and wanted to leave one lasting impression.

The duel between them was a classic when Boycott went out to open the innings with Larkins. It was a fascinating piece of cricket to watch from the ringside. As well as trying to get the better of Boycott, I also gained the impression that Lillee was trying to put one over on Alderman as well, the young upstart who had stolen most of the Australian bowling glory during the summer on his way to breaking Lillee's 31 wicket record of Test victims in England in an Ashes series.

It was never easy for Boycott. The runs he was able to score off Lillee were given away grudgingly. And Lillee was kept alive and fresh by the wickets he was able to pick up at the other end in accounting for Larkins, Tavare and Gatting, although all three made useful scores. Gatting had fallen to Lillee's first ball with the second new ball, bowled when not offering a stroke, a dismissal

---

It was quite a summer for the new boys. First Terry Alderman, then Paul Allott and then twenty-three-year-old New South Wales batsman Dirk Welham who was given his chance at The Oval and accepted it with a century in the second innings. He played with such composure to suggest he will be a regular middle order Test batsman over the next few years. And he seldom missed an opportunity to punish anything loose as he shows here when striking out boldly for the boundary

which should have brought Parker to the wicket on his debut.

Instead Mike Brearley showed a nice human touch by promoting himself one place in the order in an attempt to deal with the new ball and lessen the ordeal for Parker. Unfortunately the gesture didn't spare Parker for long. Mike got a nasty one from Alderman which bounced higher than he expected and he edged a catch to gully. He was out for a duck, the same fate awaiting Parker when he failed to move his feet and edged a ball from the same bowler into the hands of first slip.

I didn't stay long either. By the time I arrived at the crease Boycott had already reached his century, achieved when he swept Bright to the boundary for only his third four in five and a half hours at the wicket. It was his twenty-first century in Test cricket. Lillee was to have me caught in the gully for three, the same combination which eventually accounted for Boycott after he had made 137. And Lillee finally finished off the innings by bowling Knotty with a perfectly straight delivery to give him seven wickets in the innings for a cost of 89 runs off 31.4 overs. It was a glimpse of Lillee of old.

Thanks to Boycott, we had climbed to within 38 runs of Australia's total. With only just over two days left we were not thinking of victory on so perfect a batting wicket. Our only danger was if the Australians raced away in their second innings and gave themselves more than a day in which to try and bowl us out a second time. Ideally they would have liked to have had 30 minutes or so bowling at us on the fourth evening in the hope of taking a quick wicket or two. They might even have given themselves those 30 minutes but for an act of kindness by Hughes in allowing Welham to mark his first Test for his country with a century.

Although Bob Willis could only bowl 10 overs during the Australian second innings before his stomach injury forced him to go off, Hendrick was handicapped by his side strain and I was suffering from a pinched nerve in the lower buttock which caused me pain every time I moved, we still managed to prevent the Australians piling on the runs as quickly as they had hoped. They had lost Kent and Hughes on the Saturday evening in extending their first innings lead by another 36 runs. They were to lose Wood and Yallop fairly quickly on the Monday morning. It only served to bring Border and Welham together in a 101 run partnership for the fifth wicket which gave them hope of being able to declare that evening and have a go at us.

Two things forced Hughes to abandon that plan. Firstly, the twenty-two-year-old Welham became stuck in the nineties just when Hughes was hoping he would be able to gallop through them. Secondly, the skies started to darken and Hughes appreciated that any declaration would be a waste of time because Lillee and Alderman would never be allowed to bowl in the bad light.

Out in the middle Welham was deeply conscious of the plans Hughes had made in hoping to be able to declare with 40 minutes to go. It didn't help his nerves trying to find those few extra runs he needed to reach three figures. He didn't relax until I bowled Bright and Lillee came in to tell Welham – then on 99 – not to worry and to take his time because Hughes had abandoned his declaration intention. In fact his one hundredth run soon followed after almost four and a half hours at the crease, Australia going through to make 344 for nine at the close which gave them a lead of 382.

The Australian declaration came first thing on the final morning as we expected which meant that we were being set 383 to win or six hours to survive. The first objective was never on. If we had hoped for it, our minds would soon have been changed with Boycott bowled for a duck in Lillee's first over and Tavare falling to Whitney when we had only 18 on the scoreboard. Victory was never in our minds. But it began to creep into the thoughts of the Australians when we slumped to 127 for five and then 144 for six on my dismissal with a possible three hours 40 minutes remaining.

Larkins held the Australians up making 24 before Lillee accounted for him. Gatting made his fourth half-century of the series before he too went to the Australian fast bowler. Then it was Alderman's turn in claiming Parker and having me leg-before to help him set a new Australian record for an Ashes series by notching up 42 wickets.

Our predicament brought out the best in Mike who was determined that he would not bow out of Test cricket with a defeat against his name. He was determined, too, that Alec Bedser's last match as chairman of selectors would not be spoilt. He found a perfect ally in his cause in Knotty. Together they took the score to 237 for seven before Mike was beaten. By that time the Australians were in the eighth over of the last 20 and everybody could relax, although Hughes went right to the end.

The survival roles of Mike and Knotty were not without their difficult moments, Knotty suffering in particular. He gave the Australians hope by playing and missing at deliveries he should have left alone. He explained afterwards that he had become so used to batting for Kent in a position where he was expected to chase runs all the time that he felt drawn to attack every ball that came his way. After an hour at the crease he began to sort things out and was seldom in trouble, making the last 50 of his unbeaten 70.

The Australians had one final fling which might have proved disastrous for us. With 10 overs remaining they took the new ball, but Knotty and Emburey were not going to be moved at that late stage. They held out for the draw. An anti-climax, yes, but Australia had gone a long way towards restoring their cricketing reputation by the way they had fought back after the disappointments they had suffered.

And for us it had been a summer of glory, a tale of dramatic victories when all seemed lost, and the retention of the Ashes. What was more important, we had proved that there is a vast cricketing public out there waiting to be enticed back inside the grounds by a winning side. I'm sorry I could not have enticed them back during the period I was in charge but I am proud of the contribution I made towards having them flocking in at Old Trafford and The Oval when the game could once again boast that Test cricket was being played in England behind locked doors.

A memory that Dirk Welham will cherish for the rest of his life. *Opposite:* The back foot cover drive for four against me which brought him his century; (*overleaf*) the pause while the message sinks home and then (*facing page*) the raised fist to celebrate and acknowledge the cheers from his fellow Australians who had gathered on the dressing-room balcony to salute him. Two minutes later it was all over when I dismissed him leg-before in the same over

England v. Australia
SIXTH TEST

at The Oval, Thursday, Friday, Saturday, Monday 27, 28, 29, 31 Aug. & Tuesday, 1 Sept. 1931

AUSTRALIA

		First Innings		Second Innings	
1	Graeme Wood (Western Australia)	c Brearley b Botham	66	c Knott b Hendrick	21
2	Martin Kent (Queensland)	c Gatting b Botham	54	c Brearley b Botham	7
*3	Kim Hughes (Western Australia)	Hit wicket b Botham	31	lbw b Hendrick	6
4	Graham Yallop (Victoria)	c Botham b Willis	26	b Hendrick	35
5	Allan Border (Queensland)	not out	106	c Tavaré b Emburey	84
6	Dirk Wellham (New South Wales)	b Willis	24	lbw b Botham	103
‡7	Rodney Marsh (Western Australia)	c Botham b Willis	12	c Gatting b Botham	52
8	Ray Bright (Victoria)	c Brearley b Botham	3	b Botham	11
9	Dennis Lillee (Western Australia)	b Willis	11	not out	8
10	Terry Alderman (Western Australia)	b Botham	0		
11	Mike Whitney (New South Wales)	b Botham	4	c Botham b Hendrick	0

B4, l-b6, w1, n-b4, 15

Total (132 overs)... 352

B1, l-b8, w1, n-b7, 17

Total 9 wkts dec (104.2 overs)... 344

Fall of wickets—First Innings 1—120 ... 2—125 ... 3—169 ... 4—199 ... 5—260 ... 6—280 ... 7—303 ... 8—319 ... 9—319 ... 10—352

Second Innings 1—26 ... 2—36 ... 3—41 ... 4—104 ... 5—205 ... 6—291 ... 7—332 ... 8—343 ... 9—344 ... 10—

Bowling Analysis 1st Innings	O.	M.	R.	W.	Wd.	N.b.	2nd. Innings	O.	M.	R.	W.	Wd.	N.b.
Willis	31	6	91	4		4	Willis	10	0	41	0		7
Hendrick	31	8	63	0			Botham	42	9	128	4		
Botham	47	13	125	6	1		Hendrick	29.2	6	82	4	1	
Emburey	23	2	58	0			Emburey	23	3	76	1		

ENGLAND

		First Innings		Second Innings	
1	Geoffrey Boycott (Yorkshire)	c Yallop b Lillee	137	lbw b Lillee	0
2	Wayne Larkins (Northamptonshire)	c Alderman b Lillee	34	c Alderman b Lillee	24
3	Chris Tavaré (Kent)	c Marsh b Lillee	24	c Kent b Whitney	8
4	Mike Gatting (Middlesex)	b Lillee	53	c Kent b Lillee	56
*5	Mike Brearley (Middlesex)	c Bright b Alderman	0	c Marsh b Lillee	51
6	Paul Parker (Sussex)	c Kent b Alderman	0	c Kent b Alderman	13
7	Ian Botham (Somerset)	c Yallop b Lillee	3	lbw b Alderman	16
‡8	Alan Knott (Kent)	b Lillee	36	not out	70
9	John Emburey (Middlesex)	lbw b Lillee	0	not out	5
10	Bob Willis (Warwickshire)	b Alderman	3		
11	Mike Hendrick (Derbyshire)	not out	0		

B , l-b9, w3, n-b12, 24

Total (110.4 overs)... 314

B2, l-b5, w2, n-b9, 18

Total 7 wkts (95 overs)... 261

Fall of wickets—First Innings 1—61 ... 2—131 ... 3—246 ... 4—248 ... 5—248 ... 6—256 ... 7—293 ... 8—293 ... 9—302 ... 10—314

Second Innings 1—0 ... 2—18 ... 3—88 ... 4—101 ... 5—127 ... 6—144 ... 7—237 ... 8— ... 9— ... 10—

Bowling Analysis 1st Innings	O.	M.	R.	W.	Wd.	N.b.	2nd. Innings	O.	M.	R.	W.	Wd.	N.b.
Lillee	31.4	4	89	7	2	1	Lillee	30	10	70	4	1	
Alderman	35	9	84	3	1	11	Alderman	19	6	60	2		9
Whitney	23	3	76	0			Whitney	11	4	46	1	1	
Bright	21	6	41	0			Bright	27	12	50	0		
							Yallop	8	2	17	0		

*Captain   ‡Wkt.-keeper   Scorers: Jack Hill & David Sherwood   Umpires—Harold Bird & Barrie Meyer   Toss won by—ENGLAND

NEW BALL the fielding team may not claim a new ball until 85 overs have been bowled   RESULT— DRAWN

Hours of play—1st 2nd 3rd & 4th days: 11.00 a.m.—6.00 p.m. (or 7.00 p.m. in the event of weather interference)   5th day: 10.30 a.m.—5.00 or 5.30 p.m.

Lunch: 1.00—1.40 p.m. (5th day 12.30 p.m.)   Tea: 3.40—4.00 p.m. (5th day 3.10 p.m.)   (20 overs from 4.30 p.m.)

RESULTS:
1st TEST (TRENT BRIDGE)—AUSTRALIA WON BY 4 WICKETS.
2nd TEST (LORD'S)—DRAWN.
3rd TEST (HEADINGLEY)—ENGLAND WON BY 18 RUNS.
4th TEST (EDGBASTON)—ENGLAND WON BY 29 RUNS.
5th TEST (OLD TRAFFORD)—ENGLAND WON BY 103 RUNS.

CONGRATULATIONS
TO THE ENGLAND TEAM
FOR RETAINING THE ASHES.

10 We'll keep the Ashes next time

We next meet up with Australia to dispute the Ashes when we go 'down under' in November 1982, which is not too far away. I've no doubt that the Australians went home confident they could get the Ashes back during that series, despite what happened to them over here in the wonderful summer of 1981.

It is easy to understand their confidence. Although they failed in their main objective and took a hiding just when it seemed as though they were on the verge of a major triumph, they can claim they emerged from their visit with more pluses than we could register.

They will point to the astonishing success of Alderman and his record-breaking achievement on his first tour abroad. They had brought him over as a stock bowler, the man to do the donkey-work, keep the runs down while the main strike bowlers were resting in-between their spells of fury. Instead he emerged as a strike bowler himself, ideally suited to make the best of English conditions. We helped him, unfortunately, by producing wickets at Trent Bridge and Headingley that he was able to exploit to the full.

I don't think he would have made the same impact if Graham Gooch had been on top of his form and not worn out by his touring activities in the West Indies. I'm taking nothing away from Alderman but he is exactly the right kind of pace for Goochie and I'll back Goochie against him any time in the future. But where Alderman did score was in his slip catching. I can't remember him missing one all through the series and he took some beauties, making it appear much easier than they were. We will be hearing a lot more of him although I don't expect him to create so much havoc the next time we meet.

One bowler who might is Geoff Lawson, if he can build up his strength. He is genuinely quick, as he demonstrated when taking his seven wickets at Lord's in the second Test which earned him the 'Man of the Match' award for that game. He is one who could cause us trouble in 1982–83. He has a little vicious streak in him which all fast bowlers need as I discovered at Leeds with those two successive beamers. The Australians missed him over the last three Test matches but it was perhaps just as well for Lawson's sake that I didn't get him in my sights again.

Although Dennis Lillee may never make another full Test series in this country, I wouldn't be surprised if he is still around when we next go over there. Dennis got the impression I was trying to have a go at him this summer; that I had gone around saying he was over the hill. I never said that.

What I did say was that Dennis was no longer the strike bowler he used to be, despite the fact that he was still able to finish the series with 39 wickets and become the leading Australian wicket-taker in matches against England (having taken 163 wickets). I think my comment was fair enough. I was, in fact, paying him a compliment by saying how brilliantly he had adapted himself so that he still remained a considerable force in Test cricket although he had, at the age of 32, lost that extra zip which used to bring him so many wickets.

On the fast bowling front the Australians will be well served the next time we meet them. They will be well served with batsmen too. Kim Hughes, Allan Border, Graeme Wood and John Dyson should all still be around and two more have been unearthed in Martin Kent and Dirk Welham. They both made their Test debuts during the series.

Kent, tall and slim, looks the more polished player of the two, as you would expect from a batsman who has been in the Queensland side for a number of seasons and was brought up under the influence of Greg Chappell. After the way he played in the first Prudential Cup match at Lord's when making 28 – his side's second highest score – I was surprised he had to wait until the fourth Cornhill Test at Edgbaston before making his Test debut.

Welham's century in the final Test at The Oval confirmed all we had heard about him. Steady, nothing flashy, he has improved considerably in a short space of time and is a better player now than when I first came across him playing for the Combined

It was a record-breaking summer for all the four fast bowlers who were to dominate the Ashes series. Leading the way was Terry Alderman who finished his first series with 42 wickets from the six Tests, beating Dennis Lillee's record for the number of victims by an Australian in England. It also established a new record for an Australian bowler against England beating the previous record of 41 wickets set by Rodney Hogg in Australia

Universities against England in Adelaide on the 1979–80 tour. He made 95 that day, just missing out on his century when he went for a big hit in the final over in a last desperate bid to clinch a three-figure score.

Border, the gritty and stocky left-hander, was the man who caused us the most trouble, as you might expect from a batsman who averages over 50 in Test-match cricket. He was courageous throughout, scoring his two centuries when he was bothered by a broken finger. He was the mainstay of their batting, especially with his captain having a poor time with the bat.

I've no doubt they have said the same thing about Hughes back in Australia as was said about me. That he couldn't combine the job of captain and maintain his form as a player. That the strain of doing both was too much for him. He certainly ran into technical difficulties with the bat, getting himself out leg-before playing across the line. I've no doubt, too, that he has taken some terrible stick for the way he led the side in the field. They don't take too kindly to a losing captain in Australia. But I thought they went too far when the Australian cricket presenters insisted on wearing black armbands after Australia's defeats at Headingley and Edgbaston.

Personally, I thought Hughes did a good job on the field. He was very quick to learn the facts of life in limited-over cricket and generally handled the side well in the Test series. He was quite willing to accept the blame when things went wrong for Australia in the field, even when he was acting on advice from his two senior players, Dennis Lillee and vice-captain Rodney Marsh.

Off the field I thought he was a winner – blunt, honest, never ducking an issue and conducting himself like a perfect ambassador. He came across well to the general public, and those who saw the puzzled expression frozen on his face at the end of the television interview following Australia's defeat at Edgbaston will never forget it.

With Border in his present form, Hughes in the form he showed the previous year when playing in the Centenary Test at Lord's and supported by Kent and Welham, the Australians have the makings of a decent batting line-up. With Lawson to spearhead the attack supported by Alderman and Lillee, they should have a strong enough pace attack for when we next come across them. I'm not quite so sure about the rest. The wicketkeeping will be no problem as long as Marsh carries on but his batting has started to decline.

Just three wickets below Alderman was Dennis Lillee who took 11 in the final Test at The Oval in what was undoubtedly his last Test appearance in England. They helped him set a new record in becoming the leading Australian wicket-taker against England of all time with 163 victims

Above: 'Bustling Bob' the Australians nicknamed Bob Willis after he had bowled them to defeat with his eight wickets in their second innings at Heading-ley. They helped him become the leading England wicket-taker in matches against Australia with 110 victims in all. No other out-and-out fast bowler has taken 100 Australian wickets which underlines the weight of his performance

Opposite: My feat at The Oval was a personal one, picking up the eight wickets I needed to take my tally in Tests to 200 on the ground where I had become the youngest player to achieve the Test match double of 100 wickets and 1,000 runs. I had started the Test match needing just another 42 runs to score 2,000 and do the double double but finished it still 23 runs short of my target after a disap-pointing innings of three and 16 – too whacked after two long bowling stints to be able to concentrate on batting properly. One of the reasons why I believe I failed with the bat during my 12 months as England captain was that I found myself at the crease without having recovered sufficiently from my bowling stints

Spin bowling *will* be a problem. Ray Bright's left-arm spin has never particularly impressed me. I'd fancy my chances against him any day of the week. Yet I saw very little on my last Australian tour to suggest that they have anybody else at the moment to challenge him. There was no left-arm spinner or off-spinner to concern me or the rest of the England players.

The Australians can go home confident that they have found a couple of players for the future, but I'm willing to have a bet now that the Ashes will still be in England's care when we return home from Australia in the spring of 1983.

Before I leave the Australians I must add one last word of thanks to Hughes for the things he said about me at Old Trafford after we had made sure of retaining the Ashes this time: 'Anybody who attempts to change Botham in any shape or form should be locked up in gaol, the key thrown away. You people must be mad to try and change him, make him alter his style or approach.' They are exactly my sentiments, Kim!

11 Shattered

I celebrated the end of perhaps the most wonderful Ashes series there has been in modern times by doing the thing that comes most naturally to me – I went to sleep. I was so utterly and completely whacked that I carried on sleeping for almost two days with only the occasional break for a meal.

It happened at Edgbaston immediately after the final Test at The Oval. I had driven there to join my Somerset colleagues, who were playing Warwickshire in the county championship seeking a 24-point victory to keep them in the hunt for the Schweppes Pennant in case either Nottinghamshire or Sussex slipped up at the final fence. I wasn't fit enough to play. My damaged knee, which I received just before entering the final Test, was still causing me a little bother. Worse was the trapped nerve low in my left buttock. Some people suggested it was connected with the back trouble I had had the season before, but I knew that wasn't the case. It was an entirely different type of pain and it was coming from a different area.

Even if I had been physically fit to play at Edgbaston I doubt whether I would have been mentally fit. The strain of being forced to bowl 89 overs during that final Test as a result of both Bob Willis and Mike Hendrick being injured after the match had started had taken its toll. But I wanted to go to Edgbaston to give the Somerset lads a cheer in case they needed it. They beat Warwickshire without me.

I had driven up there late on the Tuesday evening after saying goodbye to my fellow England players. Some I would be meeting again in India. Others not selected would not come across me again until next summer. The end of a cricket season is always a sad business even though you are looking forward to a rest. When I arrived in Birmingham I went straight to my room and collapsed on the bed, sleeping solidly through for almost nine hours before I woke in time to drag myself down to the Warwickshire ground. Once there I just slumped in a chair not bothering to move until the dressing-room area was less crowded.

I didn't see any of the cricket. I slept practically the whole of the day on a bench in the Somerset dressing-room, coming to when the day's play had ended. Then it was out for a meal with some of the Somerset players before finding my hotel bed again around ten o'clock that evening and sleeping for another 10 hours without a murmur. From around ten on Tuesday evening until eight o'clock on the Thursday morning I estimate I must have been asleep for all but eight hours.

It was only when I recovered from that long and deep sleep that I was able to look back on the summer's Test series and slowly take it all in. What had started as a nightmare with my match-by-match trial appointment as England captain had ended like a dream. And I had lost the captaincy.

That was a personal disappointment which didn't matter when viewed in the wider context of what the summer had meant to English cricket and the defeat of the Australians which is always a good thing. I was pleased for Mike Brearley, too, the man who had come back to replace me. I think he views victory over the Australians the same way as I do. I know he had been very disappointed when we were beaten 0–3 over there during our 1979–80 tour. He had lost the England captaincy at the end of that tour because he told the selectors he would not be available to tour again. His loss was my gain. My loss during the 1981 summer was his gain, and a chance to put the record straight. Being forced to come back after taking over when we were 0–1 down made it all the harder, but it was a challenge he enjoyed.

The big question I will always ask myself is whether I could have retained the Ashes for England if I had remained in charge. I doubt whether I would have done it on a match-by-match basis because the additional pressures I experienced under that system did get to me at Lord's. But would I have been able to lead England to victory if I had been placed in charge for the complete summer? I think I would. Would I have been able to score the centuries I did in the way I did? Would I have been able to take the wickets I did taking my total aggregate over the 200 mark? I like to think I would have done.

I'm not being stubborn or silly. Other people have been more worried about my bowling form than I. I was always confident I could stay among the wickets. I know I didn't against the West Indies, but that was hardly surprising when bowling against their batting line-up. As far as my batting was concerned, I wrote earlier that I felt it was getting into shape again during the opening Test match of the series at Trent Bridge.

At the same time I have to admit I enjoyed my period of 'freedom' again, largely because it released me from all the outside pressures that had built up as a result of being put on trial before the whole country. If I had been offered the England captaincy again for the winter tour of India, it is by no means certain that I would have accepted it.

I'm quite happy to go there under Keith Fletcher. He has been around about the same number of years as Mike Brearley, thinks clearly and positively about the game, has an excellent Test record as a batsman and seems to have the knack of being able to produce a happy dressing-room, judging by what I have seen of the Essex lads. They enjoy their cricket, which is more than I can say for some other county sides. Keith will get my fullest co-operation because I shall be picking his brains out there to make sure that I shall be properly equipped for leadership when I get the chance to take over again. I say 'when' and not 'if'.

Apart from the return of my form and the pleasure of seeing Mike Brearley go out with another Ashes series win behind him, the most pleasing thing about the summer was to see Bob Willis charging in again. As Mike Brearley put it: 'He ran in like a two-year-old again instead of the carthorse he was in danger of becoming.' When he clean-bowled Lillee towards the end of Australia's first innings at The Oval, Bob – 'Bustling Bob' as the Aussies called him – became the leading wicket-taker for England against the Australians with a total of 110 victims in the 30 Tests he has played against them. He has deserved every one of them and I know the 29 wickets he picked up during the 1981 campaign gave him additional satisfaction. On his last tour to Australia in 1979–80 he struggled to find his form and the Australians were the first to write him off. They never expected to meet up with him again on a Test arena.

Hidden behind the moments of joy and delight were moments of sadness too. I mentioned Peter Willey earlier and I also had considerable sympathy for Graham Dilley who appeared to lose his way during the summer – and perhaps a bit of heart. So many people pumped him full of theory that he did not seem to know which way to turn, or what to do for the best as far as his bowling was concerned. His shoulder injury came at the worst possible moment, just when he was feeling low and unhappy with his performances.

I was delighted that the selectors remembered him when they came to name the tour party for India. Not many critics had found room for him in their idea of a tour party. He would have been one of the first names on mine. I think he'll blossom again on tour with Willis to look after him.

There was disappointment for me that Somerset did not win more and had to be content with one trophy, the Benson and Hedges. But there's always next summer to become the first county to complete a treble.

I hope I will have satisfied a personal ambition before then and obtained my private pilot's licence. Learning to fly during the 1981 summer helped me to keep my sanity during the bad periods at the start of the Ashes series. It offered me the chance to escape, to lose myself, cut myself off from the world and the problems. They just seemed to melt away. It will ease my lot appreciably when I am free to have a plane of my own, cutting down the hours I spend on the motorways travelling from match to match.

I loved it at Headingley, Edgbaston and Old Trafford when the crowd was shouting for me. I didn't mind one bit being hemmed in. But I also love it when I can get away and spend a few hours fishing or shooting, as I do as frequently as possible. Being able to fly my own plane will offer me another escape route, another safety valve and the chance to find the kind of peace I discovered again during the summer of 1981.

Appendix

Statistical highlights of the series
Recorded by Bill Frindall

FIRST TEST at Trent Bridge, Nottingham
This was the first Test match in England to include play on a Sunday. It was also the first home Test of five scheduled playing days not to include a restday. Play on the Sunday, the fourth day of the match, began at noon and ended at 5.49 p.m. when Australia completed their first victory in a Trent Bridge Test since 1948.

Not a single over of spin was bowled in the match, each side employing just four bowlers of at least medium-fast pace.

Alderman, who took nine wickets in his first Test to recall Massie's extraordinary analysis of 16 for 137 on debut at Lord's in 1972, opened his international career with a spell of 24–7–68–4 which lasted from 11.04 a.m. until 3.15 p.m.

After being stranded on 198 for eleven months, Willis at last became the sixth bowler after Bedser, Trueman, Statham, Snow and Underwood to take 200 Test wickets for England. It had taken him longer than any of the other five (10 years 5 months and 58 Tests), but only Trueman had needed fewer than Willis's 10,936 balls.

Lillee became the first Australian to take 250 Test wickets. Later in the match he took five wickets in an innings for the eighteenth time in 49 Tests. This tally equalled that of Gibbs who played 79 times for West Indies, and has been exceeded only by Barnes (24 times for England) and Grimmett (21 times for Australia).

Marsh's diving catch to dismiss Woolmer for his first 'pair' in Test cricket took Australia's vice-captain past Knott's record of 99 dismissals in Tests between England and Australia and in the same number of appearances (32). That dismissal also gave Marsh the record number of catches in Test cricket by exceeding Knott's total of 244. He ended the match with 257 dismissals in 69 Tests, needing just seven victims to claim Knott's world record set in 93 matches.

The selection of a third Chappell brother, Trevor Martin, provided the first instance of three brothers representing Australia in official Tests. This was the fifth instance of three or more brothers appearing in Test cricket, following Pakistan's four Mohammads, England's three Graces and three Hearnes and South Africa's three Tancreds.

Allowing for time made up by extending play on the second day, a net total of 5 hours 8 minutes was lost in the match.

SECOND TEST at Lord's, London

Hughes became only the second captain after Ian Chappell (1974–75) to elect to field first in successive Ashes Tests.

Boycott emulated Cowdrey by playing in one hundred official Test matches and, after batting for 240 minutes in the second innings, equalled the latter's record of 60 scores of 50 and over. Their Test career records after 100 matches make an interesting comparison:

	I	NO	HS	Runs	Avge	100	50
Boycott	177	22	246*	7,518	48.50	20	40
Cowdrey	165	15	182	7,044	46.96	21	37

(* not out)

Cowdrey also made his one hundredth appearance in a Test against Australia (at Edgbaston in 1968 when he scored 104, the last 46 being with the aid of a runner after he had pulled a hamstring), and in his thirty-fourth match against the 'old enemy'. Their respective match distributions after 100 Tests were:

	A	SA	WI	NZ	I	P
Boycott	34	7	29	15	9	6
Cowdrey	34	14	21	17	8	6

Lawson (7 for 81) recorded the third best analysis by an Australian bowler in a Test at Lord's, Massie having taken 8 for 84 and 8 for 53 in 1972.

Gatting's 59 was his highest Test score and his third fifty in four innings against Australia, while Willey's 82 ended a cheerless scoring record against that country: 9, 12, 8, 3, 1, 2, 5, 10 and 13.

Extras (55), in Australia's first innings, achieved their highest total in Tests between England and Australia. The previous record of 50 was shared, England setting it at The Oval in 1934 and Australia equalling it on the same ground four years later.

Lillee had to wait until his forty-ninth over before taking a wicket in his fiftieth Test match.

Botham's sad reign as captain of England produced four defeats and eight draws to equal their longest run of non-success in all Test matches

(Leeds 1963 to The Oval 1964). His personal record while captain presents a stark contrast to his performances before being appointed:

	M	I	NO	HS	Runs	Avge	100	50
Before	25	35	2	137	1,336	40.48	6	3
During	12	21	0	57	276	13.14	–	1

	Balls	Runs	Wkts	Avge	Best	5wI	10wM
Before	6,228	2,575	139	18.52	8–34	14	3
During	2,211	1,158	35	33.08	4–77	–	–

Allowing for time made up by extending play on the second day, a net total of 3 hours 17 minutes was lost in the match.

THIRD TEST at Headingley, Leeds
England's victory was their first in 13 Tests since they beat India in the Jubilee Match at Bombay in February 1980, and their first against Australia in seven Tests since February 1979. The margin of 18 runs was the narrowest in Ashes Tests since England won by 12 runs at Adelaide in 1928–29.

In 905 Test matches since 1877 there had been only one previous instance of a side winning after following on. On that occasion, England, under A. E. Stoddart, scored 325 and 437, beating Australia (586 and 166) by 10 runs in the First Test of the 1894–95 series at Sydney.

Brearley established a new record by leading England in nine victories against Australia, one more than W. G. Grace. For Dilley, Gatting and Willey the match provided the first savouring of victory in a collective total of 42 Test appearances.

Botham, who recorded his highest innings in Test cricket and was top scorer in both innings, scored a century and took five wickets in an innings for the fourth time in 38 Tests. This is an outstanding record; Botham apart, only Sobers and Mushtaq have achieved this feat twice; only one other player (Greig) has done so for England, and only J. M. Gregory had previously done so in Ashes Tests (100 and 7 for 69 at Melbourne in 1920–21).

Willis, 8 for 43, returned his best analysis in 60 Tests and the best by any bowler in a Test at Headingley, beating Blythe's 8 for 59 against South Africa in 1907.

Both wicketkeepers broke world records during the match. Marsh overtook Knott's record of 263 dismissals in Test cricket when he caught Botham off Lillee in the first innings. Taylor became the leading catcher in first-class cricket when he caught Lawson in the second innings and passed J. T. Murray's total of 1,270.

Lillee became the leading wicket-taker in Test matches between

Australia and England when he dismissed Willey in the second innings and passed Trumble's total of 141.

Dyson scored his second fifty in 22 Test innings, all as an opener, and went on to reach his maiden hundred and become top scorer for Australia in both innings.

After accounting for more than fifty-seven per cent of the playing time, including five complete days in the three previous Tests at Headingley (against Pakistan, India and West Indies), the Yorkshire rains claimed only a net 3 hours 22 minutes of this match.

IAN BOTHAM'S 149 NOT OUT AT HEADINGLEY

KIRKSTALL LANE END

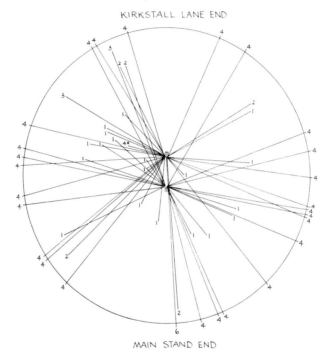

MAIN STAND END

Runs	Balls	Minutes	6s	4s
50	57	110	-	8
100	87	155	1	19
149	148	219	1	27

Bowler	Balls	Runs	6s	4s
ALDERMAN	62	68	1	11
BRIGHT	21	15	-	3
LAWSON	44	44	-	8
LILLEE	21	22	-	5

BOTHAM'S SCORING SEQUENCE

0002042000040100001000410000031
0013014204*001000404000004040400
444104000000640100040404†400010201
00010001000100400010004010420410 0
40100044100040000000.

* 4 overthrows to the mid-wicket boundary
† off a no-ball

© BILL FRINDALL 1981

FOURTH TEST at Edgbaston, Birmingham

Australia had met England at Edgbaston on only five previous occasions, winning in 1975, losing in 1909, and drawing in 1902, 1961 and 1968.

For the first time in 668 Tests since West Indies and England met on a 'sticky' pitch at Bridgetown, Barbados, in January 1935, no batsman scored a fifty.

The first session of play on the third day (Saturday) produced the slowest scoring of the series. Boycott, Gower and Gooch mustered just 37 runs in two hours off 32 overs. In that period 17 maiden overs were bowled and only 21 scoring strokes accrued from 193 balls, including a no ball.

Gower became the first Leicestershire batsman to score 2,000 runs for England when his total reached 3.

The second Sunday of Test match play in England emulated its Trent Bridge predecessor by witnessing the result of the match on the fourth day. Botham gained a 2–1 lead in the series for England and a second successive Cornhill 'Man of the Match' award for himself by returning a spell of five wickets for one run in 28 balls.

ENGLAND v AUSTRALIA 1981 — 4TH TEST

4TH DAY TIME	BOWLERS Umpires: BIRD, OSLEAR PAVILION END CITY END				BATSMEN SCOREBOARD LEFT SCOREBOARD RIGHT						NOTES	AUSTRALIA 2ND INNINGS END-OF-OVER TOTALS					
	BOWLER	O.	BOWLER	O.	SCORING	BALLS 6s/4s	SCORING	BALLS 6s/4s				O.	RUNS	W.	L BAT	R BAT	EXTRAS
					KENT	23 1	MARSH	5 1		M24 NB 13	58	114	5	6	4	14
3.50			BOTHAM	10			..W	8 1			58	114	6	6	4	14
51							BRIGHT							0		
53			.	10			W	1 .			58	114	7	6	0	14
54							LILLEE							0		
55			.	10			..	2		M25 4HR+	59					
56	EMBUREY	19			2..↑↑	27	↑+	4		† stumping appeal	60	118		9	1	
4.00			.	11	x.?.!	32	!	5		† excellent stop (Gower)	61	119		2		
04	.	20					....	11		M 26	62					
07			.	12	....	38				M 27	63					
11	.	21					.... !	17			64	120		3		
13			.	13			.W	19 .			64	120	8	9	3	14
14							HOGG							0		
16			.	13			....	4		M28	65					
19	.	22			...!↑	42	..	6		† run refused	66	121		10		
23			.	14	!.L.W	45 1				† run refused	66	121	9	10	0	14
24							ALDERMAN							0		
25			.	14	↑↑W	3 .		6 -		M 29 NB/13	67	121	10	0	0	14
4.27	ENGLAND WON BY 29 RUNS								415 balls			ALL	OUT			

BOTHAM'S MATCH-WINNING SPELL
– 5 WICKETS FOR 1 RUN IN 28 BALLS

© BILL FRINDALL 1981

FIFTH TEST at Old Trafford, Manchester
England won their third series against Australia under Brearley. His eleventh victory equalled Bradman's record in Ashes Tests.

Boycott overtook Cowdrey's record England aggregate of 7,624 runs when he hit his only boundary of the first innings. Cowdrey had played in eleven more Tests.

Alderman broke Lillee's record of 31 dismissals by an Australian bowler in England when he had Emburey caught by Border. The catch also broke Border's third finger on his left hand.

Allott marked his debut by scoring his first fifty in first-class cricket and sharing with Willis in a record tenth-wicket partnership against Australia at Old Trafford, their 56 passing the 36 by Briggs and Pilling in 1888. It was ended by Lillee, who replaced his lost record by becoming the first bowler to take 150 wickets in Anglo-Australian Tests.

Australia's 30.2 overs innings of 130 was their shortest in all Tests since 1902 when Rhodes and Hirst dismissed them for 36 in only 23 overs.

Willis, who later took three wickets in one over, took his hundredth wicket against Australia when he dismissed Dyson. He joined Peel, Barnes, Rhodes, Bedser and Underwood. In the same innings, Knott became the first wicketkeeper to make 100 dismissals against Australia.

Tavaré's second fifty of the match was the third slowest in all first-class cricket and the slowest in England. It occupied 306 minutes and was scored off 219 balls in 79 overs.

After scoring only three singles off his first 30 balls in 40 minutes, Botham reached his century off 86 balls (one fewer than at Leeds) in 104 minutes. Few of the early Test match hundreds were recorded by a method which revealed the number of balls received, but it is most probable that Botham's hundred was the second fastest for England in all Tests. Jessop reached his century against Australia at The Oval in 1902 off 75 balls. Botham's six sixes established a new record for Ashes Tests and for all Tests in England. Assisted by three runs from Tavaré, he set a new record for Test cricket in England by scoring 22 runs off one over from Lillee.

Emburey scored his first half-century in Test matches and Knott his first for England since August 1977.

Border, batting with a fractured finger, reached his hundred in 377 minutes, the slowest for Australia in 415 Tests.

Australia's total of 402 was their second-highest in a fourth innings of any Test and their highest to lose a match.

Old Trafford belied its reputation for unsocial weather: only 43 minutes were lost in the match.

IAN BOTHAM'S 118 AT OLD TRAFFORD

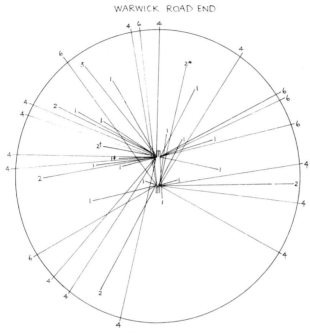

WARWICK ROAD END

STRETFORD END

Runs	Balls	Minutes	6ˢ	4ˢ
50	60	76	2	6
100	86	104	5	11
118	102	123	6	13

Bowler	Balls	Runs	6ˢ	4ˢ
ALDERMAN	17	24	1	3
BRIGHT	36	25	2	2
LILLEE	24	45	3	4
WHITNEY	25	24	-	4

BOTHAM'S SCORING SEQUENCE

```
00000011000100000000000000000000
11044104100101000000042142*161642†
24041‡460020000406004300260000
10601400400W.
```

N new ball taken at 3·37 pm (Botham 28 off 53 balls)
* dropped by WHITNEY at deep mid-off (off ALDERMAN)
† including one overthrow
‡ overthrow
W caught by MARSH off WHITNEY

© BILL FRINDALL 1981

SIXTH TEST at The Oval, London

Wood and Kent, the latter opening in a Test for the first time, recorded Australia's first century first-wicket partnership in 54 Tests since January 1977. It was also Australia's fiftieth century partnership for that wicket in all Test matches.

Australia's first innings continued to produce a flood of statistics: Brearley held his fiftieth catch in 39 Tests; Yallop scored his two-thousandth run in 58 Test innings and Hughes his one-thousandth in 31 innings against England; Border scored his second undefeated 100 in successive Test innings; Willis passed Rhodes's record of 109 wickets against Australia; Whitney scored his first runs in Test cricket and his first boundary and highest total in first-class cricket – it was only his ninth match; and Botham took five wickets in one innings for the seventeenth time in 41 Tests.

Boycott's hundred was his 124th in first-class cricket (passing Compton's total), his 21st for England (one fewer than the record shared by Hammond and Cowdrey), his seventh against Australia, and his third and highest in Tests at The Oval. He reached 1,000 runs in first-class matches for the nineteenth consecutive season and claimed Cowdrey's Test record by scoring 50 for the 61st time.

Lillee's analysis of 7 for 89 was his best in 54 Tests, beating the 6 for 26 which decided the Centenary Test at Melbourne in March 1977. By the end of the match the dismissal line, 'c Marsh b Lillee' had appeared 77 times. The next highest combination in Test cricket is 26, shared by 'c Evans b Bedser' and 'c Knott b Underwood'.

In Australia's second innings both wicketkeepers reached notable Test match milestones. Knott became the second after Marsh to hold 250 catches and Marsh became the second wicketkeeper after Knott to score 3,000 runs. After achieving his first fifty for 18 Test innings Marsh became Botham's two-hundredth Test wicket in 41 Tests – fewer than any other England bowler to take that number.

Welham became the first Australian to score a hundred on Test debut, that match being in England, since H. Graham at Lord's in 1893. The last to do so in his first Test in England was R. N. Harvey at Leeds in 1948.

Border took his aggregate against England to 313 runs in three innings, occupying 15 hours 2 minutes and 738 balls before being dismissed.

Alderman completed his first Test series by taking his 42nd wicket and breaking Hogg's record for Australia against England set in 1978–79.

Brearley's ninth 50 in 66 Test innings enabled him to retain his unbeaten record in 19 home Tests as England's captain. His successful recall had enabled England to win a home series against Australia after losing the first Test; a recovery achieved only once before, in the three-match rubber of 1888.